the handbook for
EMBEDDED
formative
assessment

Solution Tree | Press

555 North Morton Street
Bloomington, IN 47404
800.733.6786 (toll free) / 812.336.7700
FAX: 812.336.7790

email: info@SolutionTree.com
SolutionTree.com

Visit **go.SolutionTree.com/assessment** to download the free reproducibles in this book.

Printed in the United States of America

21   20   19   18   2   3   4   5

Library of Congress Cataloging-in-Publication Data

Names: Solution Tree, author.
Title: The handbook for embedded formative assessment / Solution Tree.
Description: Bloomington, IN : Solution Tree Press, 2018. | Includes
   bibliographical references and index.
Identifiers: LCCN 2017027068 | ISBN 9781945349508 (perfect bound)
Subjects: LCSH: Educational evaluation. | Educational tests and measurements.
   | Effective teaching. | Student-centered learning. | Classroom management.
Classification: LCC LB2822.75 .S64 2018 | DDC 379.1/58--dc23 LC record available at https://
lccn.loc.gov/2017027068

Solution Tree
Jeffrey C. Jones, CEO
Edmund M. Ackerman, President

Solution Tree Press
President and Publisher: Douglas M. Rife
Editorial Director: Sarah Payne-Mills
Managing Production Editor: Caroline Cascio
Art Director: Rian Anderson
Production Editor: Alissa Voss
Senior Editor: Amy Rubenstein
Copy Editor: Ashante K. Thomas
Proofreader: Miranda Addonizio
Editorial Assistants: Jessi Finn and Kendra Slayton

Table of Contents

Reproducible pages are in italics.

Introduction 1

Chapter 1
Understanding Formative Assessment 3
The Evolution of Formative Assessment 6
The Definition of Formative Assessment 9
Formative Assessment in Your Classroom 11
Formative Assessment Design 11
Strategies of Formative Assessment 13
The Bridge Between Teaching and Learning 14
Discussion Questions 16

Chapter 2
Clarifying, Sharing, and Understanding Learning Intentions and Success Criteria 17
Current Practice 17
Learning Intentions 19
Success Criteria 24
Context of Learning 30
In Your Classroom 32
Discussion Questions 35

Chapter 3
Eliciting Evidence of Learners' Achievement 37
Current Practice 37
The High-Engagement Classroom 37
High-Quality Questioning 48
In Your Classroom 54
Discussion Questions 56

Chapter 4

Providing Feedback That Moves Learning Forward 57

Current Practice 57
Feedback and the Engineering Test 57
Student Reactions to Feedback 59
Formative Feedback 65
In Your Classroom 68
Discussion Questions 70

Chapter 5

Activating Learners as Instructional Resources for One Another 71

Current Practice 71
Cooperative Learning 71
Collaboration Techniques 74
In Your Classroom 81
Discussion Questions 83

Chapter 6

Activating Learners as Owners of Their Own Learning 85

Current Practice 85
Self-Regulated Learning 85
Techniques for Student Self-Reflection 90
In Your Classroom 92
Discussion Questions 96

Appendix: Observation Tools 97

Technique Observation Template: Clarifying, Sharing, and Understanding Learning Intentions and Success Criteria 98
Technique Observation Template: Eliciting Evidence of Learners' Achievement 99
Technique Observation Template: Providing Feedback That Moves Learning Forward 100
Technique Observation Template: Activating Learners as Instructional Resources for One Another 101
Technique Observation Template: Activating Learners as Owners of Their Own Learning 102

References and Resources 103

Index 109

Introduction

As assessment expert Dylan Wiliam (2018) tells us in *Embedded Formative Assessment, Second Edition*, when educators integrate formative assessment practices into teachers' minute-to-minute and day-by-day classroom activities, substantial increases in student achievement—of the order of a 50 to 70 percent increase in the speed of learning—are possible. Moreover, these practices are not expensive to implement; classroom formative assessment is approximately twenty times as cost-effective in raising achievement as class-size reduction. In fact, we believe there is nothing else remotely affordable that is likely to have such a large effect.

Wiliam (2018) goes on to make the case for formative assessment, diving deep into the research and studies that prove formative assessment is the classroom practice with the greatest capability of increasing student achievement, and provides numerous techniques to implement formative assessment. As a companion to *Embedded Formative Assessment* (Wiliam, 2018), this handbook has one main purpose: to help you develop the practice of formative assessment in your classroom. However, this book can also act as a stand-alone resource, providing highlights directly from *Embedded Formative Assessment* as necessary for understanding and then getting straight to the how-tos of classroom formative assessment.

This handbook provides simple and practical ideas about changes that every teacher can make in the classroom to develop his or her practice of teaching. But as every teacher—and every classroom—is different, we focus on guiding you to make the changes that make the most sense for you and your students. We have endeavored to make this transition into formative assessment as easy as possible, and thus have provided several reproducible templates throughout the book for techniques that you can implement the next day. Each technique requires little in the way of technology, and you can easily adapt the techniques to use in the teaching of any subject, for any age range.

Chapter 1 outlines what formative assessment is and what it is not and presents the five key strategies of formative assessment. The remaining chapters explore each formative assessment strategy's practicalities and how to implement techniques for each. Chapter 2 discusses ways in which teachers can clarify, share, and elaborate on learning intentions and success criteria with students. Next, chapter 3 investigates how teachers can elicit evidence that gives a clear picture of what students are actually learning and achieving. Chapter 4 delves into the complex issue of feedback and provides a comprehensive look at feedback strategies that will move learning forward. Then, chapter 5 explores cooperative learning's pitfalls and positives, showing how teachers can best utilize collaboration techniques to help students help each other learn. Finally, chapter 6 discusses self-regulated learning and describes how to activate students in owning their learning. In each chapter, you will review the efficacy of your current formative assessment practices before discovering a variety of new exercises designed to guide your formative assessment implementation, as well as discussion questions to solidify your thoughts following each chapter. The appendix includes reproducible observation tools, should you be working with a colleague or teacher team.

> Rather than thinking about narrowing the gap, we should set a goal of *proficiency for all, excellence for many*, with all student groups fairly represented in the excellent. And the way to achieve this is simply to increase teacher quality. (Wiliam, 2018, p. 21)

We recommend that you work with colleagues to develop your practice; however, if you are working alone, this handbook provides the support you need to implement formative assessment in your classroom and watch your students soar. Some of the techniques may seem relatively new, but they are not. Rather, what's new is the framework that classroom formative assessment provides, which shows how the techniques fit together to have an impact on student achievement.

The problem with providing teachers with so many techniques, as psychologist Barry Schwartz (2003) points out in *The Paradox of Choice: Why More Is Less*, is that too much choice can be paralyzing—and dangerous. When teachers try to change more than two or three things about their teaching at the same time, their teaching typically deteriorates, and they revert to doing what they were doing before. We advise you to choose just a few techniques in this book and try them in your classroom. If the techniques appear to be effective, practice them until they become second nature. If they are not effective, you can modify them, or try another technique described by Wiliam (2018). No technique is likely to work for all teachers, but all teachers will, we believe, find something here that will work for them.

Remember, "the quality of an education system cannot exceed the quality of its teachers" (Barber & Mourshed, 2007, p. 19). In the United States, the effect of what classroom a student is in appears to be at least four times the size of the effect of what school a student is in (Programme for International Student Assessment [PISA], 2007), which, predictably, has generated a lot of interest in what might be causing these differences. Wiliam (2018) states:

> It turns out that these substantial differences between how much students learn in different classes have little to do with class size, how the teacher groups the students for instruction, or even the presence of between-class grouping practices (for example, tracking). The most critical difference is simply the quality of the teacher. (p. 16)

And in the most effective teachers' classrooms, students from disadvantaged backgrounds learn as much as those from advantaged backgrounds. (See, for example, Rivkin, Hanushek, & Kain, 2005; Rockoff, 2004; Sanders & Rivers, 1996.) The impact of teacher quality is, indeed, profound.

As teacher quality is the single most important variable in an education system, to improve student outcomes, we must improve the quality of teachers already in the profession. While there are many possible ways in which we could seek to develop teachers' practice, attention to minute-by-minute and day-to-day formative assessment is likely to have the biggest impact on student outcomes (see Black & Wiliam, 1998; Wiliam, 2018). Your work matters, and we present the techniques here not to give busy teachers even more work, but to help you make your work more responsive to your students' needs. So, get a pen and mark up the margins, fill out the templates, complete the exercises, and dog-ear the pages for future reference. Let's get started!

Chapter 1

Understanding Formative Assessment

Before we dive into the formative assessment strategies and practices that will shape and advance your students' learning, we must first have a thorough understanding of what formative assessment is and what it is not. Having a clear understanding of this particular process is important, especially because there are many things given the title of *formative assessment* that don't meet the definition that evidence of student achievement supports. This chapter will delve into the evolution of formative assessment and its varying definitions before looking at formative assessment in your classroom, formative assessment design, and strategies of formative assessment. It will also discuss the bridge between teaching and learning and present discussion questions for your review. But first, it will consider your existing views of formative assessment.

Let's take a quick assessment—a preassessment if you will—to determine where you are in understanding the concept of formative assessment. In figure 1.1, mark each assessment scenario as formative or summative and explain your choice in the space provided.

---

1. In spring 2016, a science curriculum supervisor needs to plan the summer workshops that the district will offer to its middle school science teachers. She analyzes the scores the district's middle school students obtained on the 2015 state tests and notes that while the science scores are generally comparable to those of the rest of the state, the students in her district appear to be scoring rather poorly on items involving physical sciences when compared with those testing life sciences. She decides to make physical science the focus of the professional development activities offered in summer 2016, which are well attended by the district's middle school science teachers. Teachers return to school in fall 2016 and use the revised instructional methods they have developed over the summer. As a result, when students take the state test in spring 2017, the achievement of middle school students in the district on items involving physical sciences increases, and so the district's performance on the state tests, which is reported in summer 2017, improves.

Source: Wiliam, 2018, pp. 43–45.

Figure 1.1: Formative assessment preassessment.

continued →

2. Each year, a group of algebra 1 high school teachers reviews students' performance on a statewide algebra 1 test and, in particular, looks at the facility (proportion correct) for each item on the test. When item facilities are lower than the group expects, the group looks at how teachers prepared and delivered instruction on that aspect of the curriculum and considers ways in which teachers can strengthen the instruction in the following year.

3. A school district administers a series of interim tests, tied to the curriculum, at intervals of six to ten weeks to check on student progress. The district uses past experience to determine a threshold that gives students an 80 percent chance of passing the state test, and requires students whose interim test scores fall below the threshold to attend additional instruction on Saturday mornings.

4. Since 2003, the School District of Philadelphia has mandated a core curriculum that includes a tightly sequenced planning and scheduling timeline, in which the school year is divided up into a number of six-week cycles (Oláh, Lawrence, & Riggan, 2010). In each six-week cycle, the district expects teachers to use the first five weeks for instruction, at the end of which students take a multiple-choice test, which the teacher can use to determine how to spend the final week of the cycle. If students have done well, teachers typically schedule enrichment and enhancement activities, but if there are significant weaknesses in students' understanding, the final week becomes a "re-teaching week" (Oláh et al., 2010).

5. A middle school science teacher is designing a unit on pulleys and levers. She allocates fourteen periods to the unit, but plans to cover all the content in the first eleven periods. Building on ideas common in the Japanese educational system (see, for example, Lewis, 2002), in period twelve, the teacher gives the students a quiz and collects the papers. Instead of grading the papers, she reads through them carefully, and based on what she discovers about what the class has and has not learned, she plans appropriate remedial activity for periods thirteen and fourteen.

6. A history teacher has been teaching about the issue of bias in historical sources. Three minutes before the end of the lesson, students pack away their books and receive an index card on which the teacher asks them to respond to the question "Why are historians concerned about bias in historical sources?" The students turn in these exit passes as they leave the class at the end of the period. After all the students leave, the teacher reads through the cards and then discards them, concluding that the students' answers indicate a good enough understanding for the teacher to move on to a new chapter.

7. A language arts teacher has been teaching his students about different kinds of figurative language. Before moving on, he wants to check his students' understanding of the terms he has been teaching, so he uses a real-time test. The teacher gives each student a set of six cards bearing the letters A, B, C, D, E, and F; and on the board, he displays the following.

   A. Alliteration

   B. Onomatopoeia

   C. Hyperbole

   D. Personification

   E. Simile

   F. Metaphor

He then reads a series of five statements.

   1. This backpack weighs a ton.

   2. He was as tall as a house.

   3. The sweetly smiling sunshine melted all the snow.

   4. He honked his horn at the cyclist.

   5. He was a bull in a china shop.

After the teacher reads each statement, he asks the class to hold up a letter card (or cards) to indicate which kind or kinds of figurative language features in each statement. All students respond correctly to the first question, but in responding to the second, each student holds up a single card (some hold up E, and some hold up C). The teacher reminds the class that some statements might be more than a single type of figurative language. Once the students realize that there can be more than one answer, the class responds correctly to statements two, three, and four. About half the students, however, indicate that they think statement five is a simile. The teacher then leads a whole-class discussion during which students give their reasons for why they think statement five is a simile or a metaphor, and after a few minutes, all the students agree that it is a metaphor, because it does not include like or as.

8. An advanced placement (AP) calculus teacher has been teaching students about graph sketching and wants to check quickly that the students grasp the main principles. She asks the students, "Please sketch the graph of $y = 1$ over $1 + x^2$." Each student sketches the graph on a whiteboard and holds it up for the teacher to see. The teacher sees that the class understands and moves on.

*Visit **go.SolutionTree.com/assessment** for a free reproducible version of this figure.*

Now, using your answers from the preassessment, define *formative assessment* (figure 1.2, page 6). Review those items that you marked as being formative. What do they have in common? Review those you marked as summative. How do they differ? What purpose does formative assessment serve? Is it a tool, a practice, an abstract concept? Be as specific and detailed as possible.

Formative assessment is:

Figure 1.2: Definition of formative assessment.

*Visit **go.SolutionTree.com/assessment** for a free reproducible version of this figure.*

> Pedagogy trumps curriculum. Or more precisely, pedagogy *is* curriculum, because what matters is *how* things are taught, rather than *what* is taught. (Wiliam, 2018, p. 12)

If you are working with a partner or a team, write out your answers individually and then work together to create a definition that you all agree on. Granted, this may be a rather tough exercise as there seem to be as many definitions of formative assessment as there are educators! It may not even be possible; in fact, it is unlikely that any definition will command universal agreement. But that's OK. This exercise is meant to get you to think about the concept of formative assessment as you understand it now. We all need a baseline from which to start our learning journey.

Now that you have clarified your thoughts regarding formative assessment, let's take a look at its evolution in the field of education.

The Evolution of Formative Assessment

Polymath and academic philosopher Michael Scriven (1967) introduces the term *formative evaluation* to describe the role that evaluation could play "in the on-going improvement of the curriculum" (p. 41). He contrasts this with summative evaluation, claiming summative evaluation's job is:

> To enable administrators to decide whether the entire finished curriculum, refined by use of the evaluation process in its first role, represents a sufficiently significant advance on the available alternatives to justify the expense of adoption by a school system. (Scriven, 1967, pp. 41–42)

Two years later, Benjamin S. Bloom (1969) applies the same distinction to classroom tests:

> Quite in contrast is the use of "formative evaluation" to provide feedback and correctives at each stage in the teaching-learning process. By formative evaluation we mean evaluation by brief tests used by teachers and students as aids in the learning process. While such tests may be graded and used as part of the judging and classificatory function of evaluation, we see much more effective use of formative evaluation if it is separated from the grading process and used primarily as an aid to teaching. (p. 48)

Bloom (1969) goes on to say, "Evaluation, which is directly related to the teaching-learning process as it unfolds, can have highly beneficial effects on the learning of students, the instructional process of teachers, and the use of instructional materials by teachers and learners" (p. 50).

Although educators used the term *formative* infrequently in the twenty years after Bloom's (1969) research, a number of researchers—and, indeed, educational practice—began to highlight the importance of using assessment to inform instruction. A number of studies were conducted to assess the power of using assessment to *adapt* instruction. In addition to these studies, several research reviews were beginning to highlight the importance of using assessment to *inform* instruction.

As the evidence that formative assessment can have a significant impact on student learning accumulates, many researchers have proposed a variety of definitions of *formative assessment*. Paul J. Black and Dylan Wiliam (1998a) define formative assessment as "encompassing all those activities undertaken by teachers, and/or by their students, which provide information to be used as feedback to modify the teaching and learning activities in which they are engaged" (p. 7). Writing around the same time, Bronwen Cowie and Beverley Bell (1999) qualify this slightly, requiring that teachers and students act upon the information from the assessment while learning takes place. Cowie and Bell (1999) define formative assessment as "the process used by teachers and students to recognise and respond to student learning in order to enhance that learning, *during the learning* [emphasis added]" (p. 32). Others also emphasize the need for action during instruction, defining formative assessment as "assessment carried out during the instructional process for the purpose of improving teaching or learning" (Shepard et al., 2005, p. 275). Reviewing practice across eight countries, the Organisation for Economic Co-operation and Development (OECD) states formative assessment is "frequent, interactive assessments of students' progress and understanding to identify learning needs and adjust teaching appropriately" (Looney, 2005, p. 21).

What is notable about these definitions is that they regard formative assessment as a process. Others regard formative assessment as a tool. For example, Stuart Kahl (2005), cofounder of Measured Progress, states formative assessment is "a tool that teachers use to measure student grasp of specific topics and skills they are teaching. It's a 'midstream' tool to identify specific student misconceptions and mistakes while the material is being taught" (p. 11). It appears educators more often use *formative assessment* to refer to a particular kind of assessment instrument than a process to improve instruction.

The difficulty with trying to make the term *formative assessment* apply to a tool or thing (the assessment itself) is that it just does not work. Consider the case of an AP calculus teacher who is getting her students ready to take their examination (Wiliam, 2018):

> Like many teachers, she has her students take a practice examination under formal test conditions. Most teachers would then collect the papers, score them, write comments for the students, and return the papers to the students so that they could see where they went wrong. However, this calculus teacher does something slightly different. She collects the papers at the end of the examination, but she does not score them. Instead, during her next period with the class, each group of four students receives its unscored papers and one blank examination paper and has to compile the best composite examination paper response that it can. Within each group, the students review their responses, comparing their answers to each question and discussing what the best answer would be. Toward the end of the period, the teacher reviews the activity with the whole class, asking each group to share its agreed-on answers with the class. (p. 40)

The AP calculus assessment that the teacher uses here was designed entirely for summative purposes. However, this teacher uses the assessment instrument *formatively*. Describing an assessment as formative is what philosopher Gilbert Ryle (1949) calls a *category error*: the error of ascribing to something a property that it cannot have, like describing a rock as happy. As Wiliam (2018) concludes, "Because the teacher can use the same assessment both formatively and summatively, the terms *formative* and *summative* make much more sense as descriptions of the *function* that assessment data serve, rather than of the assessments themselves (Wiliam & Black, 1996)" (p. 41).

Some people call to use the term *formative assessment* only when instruction improves (for example, Popham, 2006; Shepard, 2008). In the United Kingdom, the Assessment Reform Group (ARG) argues that using assessment to improve learning requires five elements to be in place (as cited in Broadfoot et al., 1999).

1. Providing effective feedback to students

2. Actively involving students in their own learning

3. Adjusting teaching to take into account the assessment results

4. Recognizing the profound influence assessment has on students' motivation and self-esteem, both of which are crucial influences on learning

5. Needing students to be able to assess themselves and understand how to improve

ARG suggests that *formative assessment*—at least in the way many people use it—is not a helpful term for describing such uses of assessment because, as it says, "the term 'formative' itself is open to a variety of interpretations and often means no more than that assessment is carried out frequently and is planned at the same time as teaching" (Broadfoot et al., 1999, p. 7). Instead, ARG suggests that it would be better to use the phrase *assessment for learning*, a term first used by Peter J. Mittler (1973) but which Mary James (1992) and Rick J. Stiggins (2001, 2005) brought to a wider audience.

> As W. Edwards Deming is reputed to have said, "In God we trust. All others bring data." (Wiliam, 2018, p. 42)

For many years, educators in the United States used the term *formative assessment* to describe a process for monitoring student achievement. Students took assessments at regular periods (typically every four to ten weeks), and teachers then looked at the resulting data to determine which students were making sufficient progress and which were not. It is important to realize that monitoring student progress is a good thing to do. However, if formative assessment merely identifies which students are falling behind, the impact on student achievement is limited. It is in response to this limited view of formative assessment that Stiggins (2005), an advocate for the term *assessment for learning* and founder of the Assessment Training Institute, writes:

> If formative assessment is about more frequent, assessment FOR learning is about continuous. If formative assessment is about providing teachers with evidence, assessment FOR learning is about informing the students themselves. If formative assessment tells users who is and who is not meeting state standards, assessment FOR learning tells them what progress each student is making toward meeting each standard while the learning is happening—when there's still time to be helpful. (pp. 1–2)

However, simply replacing the term *formative assessment* with the term *assessment for learning* merely clouds the definitional issue (Bennett, 2009). The problem, as researcher Randy E. Bennett (2009) points out, is that it is an oversimplification to say that formative assessment is *only* a matter of process or *only* a matter of instrumentation. Good processes require good instruments, and instruments are useless unless teachers are able to use them intelligently. What really matters is the kind of processes we value, not what we call them. We have considered all these issues in devising a definition of *formative assessment* for the purposes of this handbook.

The Definition of Formative Assessment

The original meaning of the word *formative*, according to *Merriam-Webster's Online Dictionary*, is "capable of alteration by growth and development" ("formative," 2017). This suggests that formative assessment should shape instruction—for example, our formative experiences are ones that shape our current selves. Thus, we need a definition that can accommodate all the many ways in which assessment shapes instruction. We base the formative assessment strategies and practices in this handbook on Wiliam's (2018) following definition:

> An assessment functions formatively to the extent that evidence about student achievement is elicited, interpreted, and used by teachers, learners, or their peers to make decisions about the next steps in instruction that are likely to be better, or better founded, than the decisions they would have made in the absence of that evidence. (p. 48)

The first point about this definition is that it uses the term *formative* to describe the function that evidence from the assessment actually serves, rather than the assessment itself. As a result, *any* assessment can thus be formative, depending on the function of the data it elicits.

The second point considers who is actually doing the assessment. While in many cases, the teachers make decisions, Wiliam's definition also includes individual learners or their peers as agents in making such decisions.

The third point is that the definition focuses on decisions instead of on the intentions of those involved, as is the case with some definitions of *assessment for learning*. Evidence that teachers collect with the intent of using, but never actually end up using, is unhelpful.

The fourth point aligns with the third, in that the focus is on the resulting *action* instead of the intent. As stated earlier, some definitions require that teachers use the evidence to make adjustments that actually improve learning beyond what would have otherwise happened without those adjustments. This, however, would make the definition of formative assessment much too stringent. Learning is too unpredictable to ever guarantee that learning will take place on a particular occasion. Moreover, if we require the assessment to result in better learning than will occur without it, it will be impossible to establish that any assessment was ever formative, since we would need to establish a counterclaim: that what actually happened is different (and better) than what will otherwise happen (but does not). The probabilistic formulation in Wiliam's definition—that the decisions are *likely* to be better—reflects the fact that even the best-designed interventions will not *always* result in better learning for *all* students.

The fifth point is that the definition focuses on decisions about the next steps in *instruction*. In the English-speaking world, the word *instruction* frequently connotes training or transmission approaches to teaching. Here, the term *instruction* refers to a combination of teaching and learning, or to any activity that intends to create learning (defined as an increase, brought about by experience, in the capacities of an individual to act in valued ways).

The sixth point is that decisions are either better *or* better founded than decisions made without the evidence that the assessment process elicits. With the second possibility, the formative assessment might indicate to the teacher that the best course of action is what the teacher had intended to do all along. The formative assessment might not change the course of action but instead simply show the teacher that the proposed course of action was right after all.

Everything a teacher does is teaching. That's all the teacher can do. *Learning* is the name we give to the rather mysterious process that occurs in students' heads, when they can do things that they were not able to do before.
(Wiliam, 2018, p. 54–55)

Now, let's look again at your definition of formative assessment and see how it compares to the definition we use in this book. Figure 1.3 contains this book's definition in the first column. Write your definition from figure 1.2 in the second column, then compare and contrast the two definitions. How did your definition differ from ours? What does your definition need to add or let go of to fully embrace the practice of formative assessment as we explain here? To make the best use of the strategies in this book, we need to share and agree on an understanding not just of formative assessment as a whole but also of its components and how they work together to raise student achievement. If you are working with others, discuss the similarities and differences between your definitions and ours and the ways these differences can impact the instruction in your classrooms.

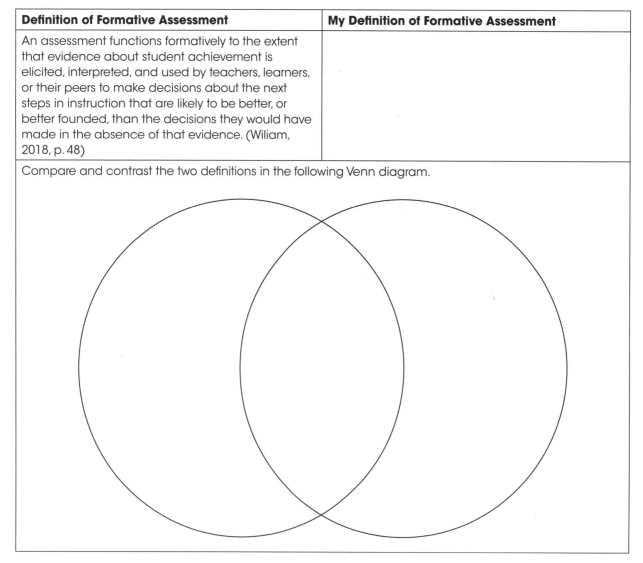

Definition of Formative Assessment	My Definition of Formative Assessment
An assessment functions formatively to the extent that evidence about student achievement is elicited, interpreted, and used by teachers, learners, or their peers to make decisions about the next steps in instruction that are likely to be better, or better founded, than the decisions they would have made in the absence of that evidence. (Wiliam, 2018, p. 48)	

Compare and contrast the two definitions in the following Venn diagram.

Figure 1.3: Analysis of interpretations of formative assessment.

Visit **go.SolutionTree.com/assessment** for a free reproducible version of this figure.

Formative Assessment in Your Classroom

As you work through the varying definitions of formative assessment, you may recognize your own instruction strategies and techniques in them. It is likely that you are already doing many things to work toward the goals formative assessment envisions. As mentioned previously, this book isn't meant to overwhelm you with another charge of to-dos. Instead, we want to work with the practices you are currently using to step up student achievement. Throughout, you will gather several ideas and new approaches to your instruction. While they will each add an element of formative assessment that will benefit the teaching and learning in your classroom, we recommend trying to implement only a few at any one time to avoid frustration and give your students the best chance of success.

Perhaps you already have formative assessment practices that will mesh well with some of the techniques we offer here. Let's take stock of what you are currently doing. List any practice you consider to be formative assessment, whether it is an exercise for just one lesson or one that you administer regularly, in the first column of figure 1.4 (page 12).

Let's now scrutinize those practices under the spotlight of our definition. In the second column, mark each practice with either a check mark (✓) or a cross (X), depending on whether or not the practice meets our definition. For those practices marked with an X, brainstorm ways to tweak that practice to fulfill formative assessment's demands. Enlist the help of your colleagues if working in a team. While we will certainly introduce several formative assessment techniques in the upcoming chapters, it is helpful to begin to think of formative assessment in terms of your own current instruction. You know your students best and therefore what practices will work best with them.

Formative Assessment Design

As stated earlier, formative assessment involves assessments that educators use to elicit evidence of student achievement and make better decisions about the next steps in instruction. The emphasis on decisions being at the heart of formative assessment assists with the assessment design process. Many so-called formative assessments generate and then communicate data to teachers, with teachers expecting that they will be able to use the information in some way. However, if educators design the formative assessments without any clear decision in mind, then there is a good chance that the information from the assessment will be useless.

For example, many vendors now offer schools regular student testing (typically every four to ten weeks), and then feed the results back to teachers. Sometimes these vendors report the results simply in terms of which students are on target to reach proficiency on the state tests and which are not, but even when the results are more detailed, they are often of little use to the teachers for two reasons. First, the results are usually at the level of state or provincial standards, which are generally too coarse to guide teachers' instructional decision making. Second, the results usually arrive weeks after the teacher moves on to a different topic of study, meaning that any information about which students may need additional help in a certain area is now useless. Caroline Wylie and Dylan Wiliam (2006) describe

> Even the best teachers fail. Talk to these teachers, and no matter how well the lesson went, they always can think of things that didn't go as well as they would have liked, things that they will do differently next time. . . . The only teachers who think they are successful are those who have low expectations of their students. (Wiliam, 2018, p. 29)

Formative Assessment Practices	Meets the Definition	Tweak the Practice

Figure 1.4: Inventory of current formative assessment practices.

*Visit **go.SolutionTree.com/assessment** for a free reproducible version of this figure.*

this kind of formative assessment as *data-push*: data are pushed at teachers; and although those designing the assessments aren't really clear about what the teacher should do with the information, they expect the teacher to be able to use these data.

The alternative, and the ideal method of formative assessment design, is to design the assessments backward from the decision. When the focus is on the decision that the teacher needs to make, he or she can then look at relevant sources of evidence that would contribute to making that decision in a smarter way. With this *decision-pull* approach, the teacher always knows what to do with these data once he or she collects them because that decision was thought through *before* he or she conducted the assessment. In this way, the teachers have planned for these specific data, receiving these data while there is still time to address them in the classroom. However, when teachers must dig through the data that result from a data-push to find what may possibly fit their needs, most likely the window for intervention has already closed.

In some ways, backward design makes creating the assessments easier; and as we'll see in the upcoming chapters, following the formative assessment strategies the next section outlines narrows down the plethora of design options you have. The endgame is student understanding and achievement. If you stay focused on that, backward design of formative assessment falls into place.

Strategies of Formative Assessment

The discussion thus far has established that any assessment can be formative, and that assessment functions formatively when it improves the instructional decisions that teachers, learners, or learners' peers make. These decisions can be on-the-fly decisions, or longer term. However, if we want to really see what formative assessment looks like in action, we have to dig a little deeper.

All teaching really boils down to three key processes and three roles. The processes are: (1) identifying where learners are going, (2) finding out where learners are in their learning, and (3) working out how to get them to their goal. The roles are: (1) teacher, (2) peer, and (3) learner. Crossing the roles with the processes produces a three-by-three grid of nine cells (see figure 1.5), which we group into five key strategies of formative assessment with one big idea (Leahy, Lyon, Thompson, & Wiliam, 2005).

	Where the Learner Is Going	Where the Learner Is Right Now	How to Get There
Teacher	Clarifying, sharing, and understanding learning intentions and success criteria	Eliciting evidence of learning	Providing feedback that moves learning forward
Peer		Activating learners as instructional resources for one another	
Learner		Activating learners as owners of their own learning	

Source: Adapted from Leahy et al., 2005.

Figure 1.5: The five key strategies of formative assessment.

The big idea is that teachers can use evidence about learning to adjust instruction to better meet student needs—in other words, teaching is *adaptive* to the learner's needs. The five key strategies are (Wiliam, 2018):

1. Clarifying, sharing, and understanding learning intentions and success criteria

2. Eliciting evidence of learning

3. Providing feedback that moves learning forward

4. Activating learners as instructional resources for one another

5. Activating learners as owners of their own learning (p. 52)

Over the next five chapters, we discuss each strategy in greater detail. Before moving on, however, it is worth considering why assessment should occupy such a central position in teaching.

The Bridge Between Teaching and Learning

To state it bluntly, students do not learn what we teach. If they did, we would have no need to keep gradebooks. We could, instead, merely record what we have taught. But anyone who has spent time in a classroom knows that what students learn as a result of our instruction is unpredictable. We teach what we think are good lessons, but then, after we collect our students' work, we wonder how they could misinterpret what we said so completely.

> We often mix up teaching and learning, as the following old joke shows.
>
> **Amy:** I taught my dog to whistle.
>
> **Betty:** Let's hear it then.
>
> **Amy:** He can't whistle.
>
> **Betty:** I thought you said you taught him to whistle.
>
> **Amy:** I did. He just didn't learn it. (Wiliam, 2018, p. 54)

As Wiliam (2018) states, "The teacher's job is not to transmit knowledge, nor to facilitate learning. It is to engineer effective learning environments for the students" (p. 55). The key features of effective learning environments are that they:

- Create student engagement

- Allow teachers, learners, and learners' peers to ensure that the learning is proceeding in the intended direction

The only way to do this is through assessment. This is why assessment is *the* central process in instruction. This is why assessment is, in fact, the bridge between teaching and learning.

Let's go back to figure 1.1 (page 5). Take a look at your answers. After reading this chapter, are there any answers you'd like to change? Do you now have a different view of formative assessment?

In each of these eight examples, the teachers use evidence to elicit and interpret student achievement to make a decision about what to do next. The length of the decision cycle varies, from years to moments. In most of the examples, the teacher decides to adjust his or her instruction to better meet the class's learning needs, and the assessment allows the teachers to make smarter decisions than would have been possible had they not collected the evidence. In examples six and eight, however, the teacher discovers that the students understand what she wants them to learn well enough for them to move on; the decision is that no adjustment is necessary. A good definition of *formative assessment* will have to admit all these as examples of formative assessment.

That being said, not all forms of formative assessment are equal. Examples six, seven, and eight are what we might call short-cycle formative assessment, because the cycle length is from minute to minute and day by day, and the impact is less on generating data and more on helping teachers respond in real time to their students' learning needs. Because these processes collect evidence from all students, rather than just those who are happy to volunteer, they increase student engagement. Such short-cycle formative assessments are what we will focus on in this book.

Although researchers have proposed many different definitions of formative assessment, the essential idea is simple. Teaching is a *contingent* activity. We cannot predict what students will learn as a result of a particular sequence of instruction. Formative assessment involves getting the best possible evidence about what students have learned and using this information to decide what to do next.

Discussion Questions

You may answer the following questions independently or with your team to reinforce the chapter's key points.

1. In your own words, describe formative assessment in the classroom.

2. What are the five strategies of formative assessment, and how do they relate to each other?

3. What is the process for assessment design in your classroom and school? Do the formative assessments reflect a *data-push* or *decision-pull* approach?

4. In what ways do you currently use formative assessment in your classroom? Are these techniques successful? Why, or why not?

Chapter 2

Clarifying, Sharing, and Understanding Learning Intentions and Success Criteria

I t seems obvious that students would find it helpful to know what they are going to be learning, and yet, consistently and effectively sharing learning intentions with students is a relatively rare phenomenon in classrooms. While many districts mandate that teachers post a learning objective to begin a lesson, this typically results in the teacher writing the objective on the board, the students copying the objective into their notebooks, and the students subsequently ignoring the objective for the rest of the period. This kind of tokenistic approach is not sufficient for sharing learning intentions and is most definitely not what the strategy of *clarifying, sharing, and understanding learning intentions and success criteria* intends.

So how, then, are students supposed to effectively understand learning intentions and success criteria? This chapter reviews some effects of ensuring learners understand what they are meant to do and explains why it is helpful to distinguish among learning intentions, success criteria, and the context of the learning. The chapter also provides a number of techniques that teachers can use to share learning intentions and success criteria with their students. Before we discuss ways to strengthen our communication of learning intentions and success criteria, let's take a look at current practices.

Current Practice

In the first column of figure 2.1 (page 18), write down the ways in which you *clarify* learning intentions and success criteria. How do you ensure your learning intentions are direct, clear, and easy for your students to understand? Perhaps you rewrite the learning intentions in jargon-free language appropriate to your students' ages. Or maybe you consider questions your students may have about the learning intentions and think about how you would explain them. Additionally, add some notes on how you decide to measure whether students have been successful in achieving the learning outcomes. You might use rubrics (created

Clarifying	Sharing	Understanding

Figure 2.1: Inventory of current practice for the strategy of clarifying, sharing, and understanding learning intentions and success criteria.

*Visit **go.SolutionTree.com/assessment** for a free reproducible version of this figure.*

yourself or in conjunction with colleagues), test the concept in a different context, or have students analyze the work of peers.

Next, in figure 2.1, write down the ways in which you *share* learning intentions and success criteria with your classes. Perhaps you include the learning intentions in the syllabi. Maybe you provide rubrics with each assignment. Possibly, you discuss the lesson's intent with your class before, during, or after the lesson. Maybe you combine all these and add more.

Finally, in the third column, note all the ways in which you ensure that your students *understand* these learning intentions and success criteria. Perhaps you ask for a show of hands of those who understand the learning intention. Maybe in your classroom students are responsible for their own learning, and you expect them to alert you to their confusion. Or perhaps you rely on assessments to tell you whether individual students understood what they were to learn.

Before delving into some strategies to help you in your practice, we will consider the differences between learning intentions and success criteria and look at the effect of the context of learning on these variables.

Learning Intentions

Professional Development Service for Teachers (2016) states that a *learning intention* "for a lesson or series of lessons is a statement, created by the teacher, that describes clearly what the teacher wants the students to know, understand, and be able to do as a result of learning and teaching activities" (p. 34). Teachers have to be able to distinguish between the learning intentions and the instructional activities that they hope will result in those outcomes, and this is a distinction that many teachers find hard to make. When asked about the learning intentions for a lesson, teachers often treat the learning intention as an activity: "I'm going to have the students do this." This is a common misconception. While lesson activities are certainly important in helping the students absorb the lesson, the lesson itself, and the activities it involves, is not the learning intention. The learning intention is what we want our students to have learned at the end of the lesson.

> Often, what teachers want is not made clear, and this puts some students at a considerable advantage because *they already know.*
> (Wiliam, 2018, p. 58)

Not all students have the same idea as their teachers about what they are meant to be doing in the classroom. As an example, we might ask students which is the odd one out in the following list of objects: knife, fork, hammer, bottle of ketchup. Some students will say that the ketchup is the odd one out because the others are all metal tools. Others will say that the hammer is the odd one out because they can find the other objects on their kitchen table at mealtime. In an absolute sense, neither of these two answers is better than the other, but as sociologist Nell Keddie (1971) points out, schools place a greater value on the first way of thinking about the world than the second. Sometimes schools make this explicit, but often, what they want isn't clarified. Students cannot succeed if they do not know what the teacher considers success.

Given this, it is not surprising that assessment expert D. Royce Sadler (1989) writes:

> The indispensable conditions for improvement are that the student comes to hold a concept of quality roughly similar to that held by the teacher, is continuously able to monitor the quality of what is being produced during the act of production itself, and has a repertoire of alternative moves or strategies from which to draw at any given point. (p. 121)

While there could be some discussion about whether, as Sadler (1989) claims, any improvement is impossible unless the conditions he specifies are met, there seems to be little doubt that it is a good idea to make sure that students understand the learning intentions behind the activities they undertake in the classroom.

But how do we do this? First, we start at the end—with backward design, as previously mentioned. We cannot tell the students what their destination is if we don't know ourselves where we want them to be at the end of the journey. So, what do we want the students to learn? What do we want the outcome of our lesson to be? Perhaps this is a specific standard the students must meet. Possibly we need to review a concept taught last year to ensure all students are on a level playing field. Whatever it is, we need to clarify the learning intention into a specific and measurable goal. For example, "Students will learn how to develop a well-designed argument" is a less effective learning intention than "Students will identify an issue, develop an arguable thesis about the issue, locate relevant supporting evidence, analyze the evidence, and draw a well-supported conclusion." Keep in mind that the intention should be conceptual rather than tied to a specific task or project.

When clarifying learning intentions, remember that we can't expect our students to meet the goals we set for them if they don't understand what we are asking for. State and provincial standards are often written in rather formal language, and it is not particularly easy for students (or teachers!) to work out what they mean. As a result, some authors advocate that teachers should adapt the state or provincial standards and present them to students in student-friendly language. Simply reading a standard from the curriculum guide isn't going to do much good if students aren't privy to the academic vocabulary.

Next, we must decide at what point during the lesson we want to share the learning intention. For example, sometimes we want to be clear right from the beginning what the lesson's goals are. We may be very explicit in our expectations, such as when we require laboratory reports to be structured in a particular way—draw diagrams and label them in pencil, and so on. At other times, it's not a good idea to tell the students what the lesson is about. Sometimes telling the students where they are going completely spoils the journey! Indeed, in conversations with students, many have said that always receiving the objectives at the start of the day turns them off. Starting a lesson with a problem that will demonstrate the learning intention without telling them (think *showing* instead of *telling*) can be a great way to grab the students' attention, and the mystery surrounding the outcome supports motivation. Consider the problem in figure 2.2, suitable for a middle school mathematics class.

Two farmers have inherited adjacent fields with a boundary that has a kink in it:

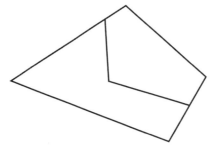

Both farmers find the crooked boundary to be an inconvenience, and so they wonder whether it is possible to divide the two fields with a straight boundary so that each farmer still has the same amount of land.

Source: Wiliam, 2018.

Figure 2.2: "Two Fields" mathematics problem.

There are, of course, numerous ways in which such a problem might be solved, but one key insight that simplifies the problem considerably is that triangles with equal bases and height must have the same area (because the formula for the area of a triangle is ½ × base × height). So if a straight line is drawn between the points where the boundary meets the edge of the fields, and a parallel line is drawn through the kink in the boundary, any triangles with a base on the line between the boundary points and the third corner on the parallel line will have the same area (see figure 2.3). Therefore, either of the two heavy lines on the diagram in figure 2.4 will do.

This problem would have been completely pointless if the teacher had told the students at the outset that they were learning to solve problems involving the area of a triangle. Once students realize that the area of a triangle is relevant, the problem is relatively simple to solve.

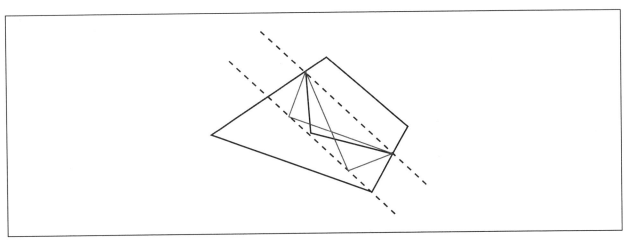

Source: Wiliam, 2018.

Figure 2.3: Working for the "Two Fields" problem.

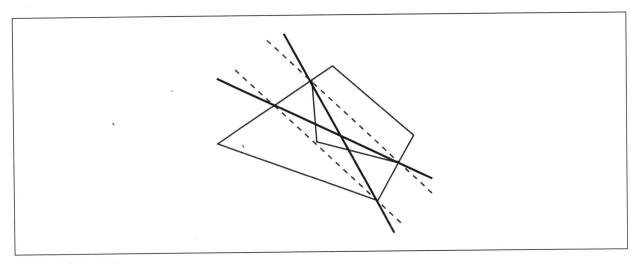

Source: Wiliam, 2018.

Figure 2.4: Solution for the "Two Fields" problem.

It is often valuable to develop the learning intentions jointly with students—a process that is sometimes called *co-construction*. It is important to note that developing learning intentions or success criteria with students is most definitely not a democratic process. The teacher is in a privileged position and knows more about the subject than the students do, and the teacher would be abdicating his or her responsibilities to adopt whatever the students feel should be valued as the learning intentions. The advantage of developing the learning intentions with the students is that doing so creates a mechanism whereby students can discuss and come to own the learning intentions and success criteria, making it more likely that they will be able to apply the learning intentions and success criteria in the context of their own work. For an example of how to co-construct success criteria, see Sample Student Work on page 28.

Back in 1971, Mary Alice White tried to imagine "the view from the student's desk":

> The analogy that might make the student's view more comprehensible to adults is to imagine
> oneself on a ship sailing across an unknown sea, to an unknown destination. An adult would be

desperate to know where he is going. But a child only knows he is going to school. . . . The chart is neither available nor understandable to him. . . . Very quickly, the daily life on board ship becomes all important. . . . The daily chores, the demands, the inspections, become the reality, not the voyage, nor the destination. (p. 340)

> Good teaching is so extraordinarily difficult. It is relatively easy to think up cool stuff for students to do in classrooms, but . . . too often, it is not clear what the students are going to learn. It is also relatively easy . . . to stand at the front of the class and lecture students on what you want them to learn, but many students do not learn well with such an approach. (Wiliam, 2018, pp. 66–67)

Taking White's advice, let's look at our learning intentions from our students' perspective. In the first column of figure 2.5, write down five learning intentions. Let this worksheet work for you. Choose five that your students struggle with every year, or choose the learning intentions for the next five lessons to help you get a jumpstart on them.

Now consider each of the five from your students' perspective. Is there academic language that requires explanation? Is each learning intention a complex sentence with many parts? Does each learning intention work only in the classroom, or does it transfer easily to real-world applications? In the second column, rewrite the learning intentions in language your students will understand. For instance, if you have younger students, you may want to begin the learning intention with "I will be able to . . .," and conclude the sentence with the end goal you have for this lesson.

If you are working with a grade-level team, share this exercise and discuss. One of your best resources is your colleagues. Collaborating on learning intentions and success criteria will help to ensure that all students in the grade are learning the same thing regardless of the teacher they have.

It is also worth remembering that the standards' language often characterizes the discipline that the standards represent. Students might not understand what the term *sense of audience* means, and one response might be to try to express the meaning in simpler words, but it is also important that students begin to understand the phrase *sense of audience* as a term of art in language arts. Student-friendly language can be useful as educators introduce students to a discipline, but it is also important to help students develop the habits of mind that define the discipline, and coming to terms with the "official" language is part of that process. Keep this in mind as you share the learning intentions with students.

> Some students already know what successful work looks like, and others do not. Ensuring that all students know what quality work looks like has a profound impact on achievement gaps. (Wiliam, 2018, p. 61)

Now that you have a few student-friendly learning intentions, what are you going to do with them? Many educators find it beneficial to post a learning intention somewhere accessible in the classroom, so teachers can point to it, and students can see it throughout the lesson. Indeed, some districts require this. It is not enough, however, to simply post the learning intention for all to see or to have students repeat an "I will be able to . . ." sentence as a means of sharing the intention with students. Educators must be sure that students *understand* both what the learning intention means and what the learning intention looks like to fully share the learning intention. This is where success criteria come in.

Learning Intention	Student-Friendly Rewrite
1. Learn how to convert C temp to F. between measurement systems	Students write convert c to F using the formula give
2. Learn 10 feeling vocab words	Students will speak, write, pronounce 10 voc. words in the correct grammatical sequence
3. → Business ethics develop an idea →	
4. maintain a social conversation	
5.	

Figure 2.5: How to communicate learning intentions using student-friendly language.

Visit **go.SolutionTree.com/assessment** *for a free reproducible version of this figure.*

Success Criteria

Success is the manifestation of a learning intention. Success isn't an A, although that could very well be the grade the work receives. Additionally, success isn't simply memorizing and regurgitating information—except in rare cases where knowing number facts is the sole success criterion. More commonly, success is learning—learning the concept being taught and being able to transfer that learning to a context outside the classroom. As you can imagine, creating criteria for such success can be rather challenging, if not outright difficult. *Success criteria* "are developed by the teacher and/or the student and describe what success looks like. They help the teacher and student to make judgements about the quality of student learning" (Professional Development Service for Teachers, 2016, p. 34). For example, figure 2.6 provides success criteria for a learning intention in writing.

Learning intention: Present a point of view in a persuasive manner.
Success criteria:
• Begin with an attention-grabbing opening sentence.   • Present reasons and examples to back up your argument.   • Use emotive and persuasive language (such as "Surely").   • Use humor, stories, questions, or all of these to keep your audience's attention.   • Conclude with a strong statement.   • Consider your audience.

Source: Adapted from National Council for Curriculum and Assessment, 2015.

Figure 2.6: Example of learning intention with success criteria.

Look back to figure 2.1 (page 18). What are some ways that you share success criteria with your students? Take a moment to think about, or discuss with your teaching team, practices for ensuring students understand what you expect of them. Keep in mind that when we are in summative mode, success criteria should determine the extent to which students have been successful. When we are in formative mode, success criteria should bring about that success.

Now, fill out figure 2.7 using one of your learning intentions from figure 2.5 (page 23).

In completing this exercise, we may come to find that we are quite comfortable with the idea of giving students clear guidance about what we want, but defining success criteria turns out to be too difficult. We sometimes use learning objectives as if they are definitions of quality when in fact they are post-hoc rationalizations of quality—familiar enough to those who know what they are doing, but not helpful to those who are not yet there. To overcome this difficulty, effective success criteria should be measurable, allow for differentiation between students, be expressed in clear and meaningful language, and allow students to identify success for themselves. In addition, teachers should provide examples of work that meet the success criteria.

Another step we can take to ensure our students understand success is to help the students develop what Guy L. Claxton (1995) calls a *nose for quality*, meaning learners instinctively know what good quality means and looks like. If students have a nose for quality, they are much better able to work toward meeting success

Learning intention:
Success criteria:

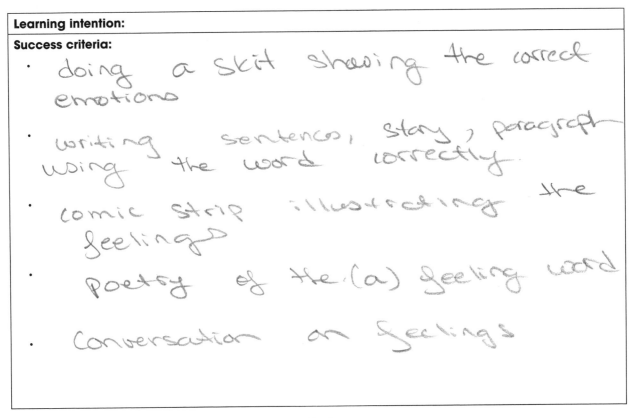

- doing a skit showing the correct emotions

- writing sentences, story, paragraph using the word correctly.

- comic strip illustrating the feelings

- Poetry of the (a) feeling word

- Conversation on feelings

Figure 2.7: Learning intention with success criteria.

*Visit **go.SolutionTree.com/assessment** for a free reproducible version of this figure.*

criteria without the confusion that can hinder achievement. We will now investigate three tools teachers can use for developing this skill in students.

1. Rubrics

2. Process criteria

3. Sample student work

Rubrics

When students are given time to think through, in discussion with others, what a rubric might mean in practice and as it applies to their own work, a rubric can be an effective instrument for sharing success criteria. There are several ways to create rubrics, and a teacher's own creativity is his or her only limit. A scoring rubric—which is really just a way of presenting success criteria—can be task specific, so that it applies to just a single task, or it can be generic, so that teachers can apply the same rubric to a number of different tasks (see Stiggins, 2001).

Task-specific rubrics can be written in very clear language to communicate accurately to students what that particular task requires, but this strength is also a weakness in that only the specific tasks define success. By being specific about what we want, we can focus students' learning too much, instead of encouraging transferable skills. An additional weakness of task-specific rubrics is that students must come to grips with a new rubric for each task. Judith A. Arter and Jay McTighe (2001) suggest that task-specific rubrics are generally more appropriate for summative assessment. Specific criteria are useful when we want students to know exactly what we want them to demonstrate. They make sure students know what we are looking for, and thus they are useful at the end of learning.

> What matters most is not what teachers put into the rubric, but what the students get out of it. (Wiliam, 2018, p. 74)

During learning, however, it is helpful to build a degree of generality into scoring rubrics so as to promote transfer. Generic rubrics focus on the learning intention rather than the activity, or task, meant to support the learning intention. As Alfie Kohn (2006) points out, scoring rubrics that are too detailed can be counterproductive. If you specify in detail what students are to achieve, then they may well achieve it, but that is probably all they will be able to do. As Wiliam (2018) states, "The clearer you are about what you want, the more likely you are to get it, but the less likely it is to mean anything" (p. 66).

According to professor of education and consultant Susan M. Brookhart (2013), generic rubrics have several advantages over task-specific rubrics, especially when it comes to formative assessment. Brookhart (2013) says general rubrics:

- Can be shared with students at the beginning of an assignment, to help them plan and monitor their own work.
- Can be used with many different tasks, focusing the students on the knowledge and skills they are developing over time.
- Describe student performance in terms that allow for many different paths to success.
- Focus the teacher on developing students' learning of skills instead of task completion.
- Do not need to be rewritten for every assignment.

If you currently use rubrics in your classroom, take a moment to identify their uses. Do you use them more often in a formative or summative way? Using success criteria from figure 2.7 (page 25), let's build a rubric to help students understand what success looks like (see figure 2.8). If you are working with a colleague or team, share your rubric and ask for feedback from the student perspective. Are there questions about the definitions of quality? Perhaps the rubric is a bit too specific, limiting the learning to a particular scenario. Use the feedback to make changes to your rubric.

Process Criteria

Most learning intentions and success criteria focus on what you expect students to be able to *do* at the end of a period of instruction. This is natural because, as noted previously, the best learning needs to be designed backward from the intended destination. However, in the same way that during a road trip, it is helpful and reassuring to inform the driver that he or she is on the right track (for example, "You will pass a gas station on the left"), *process criteria*, or criteria that indicate that one's work is progressing toward these success criteria, can be useful too.

Process criteria are particularly important in helping students become owners of their own learning. If the teacher has spent some time helping students develop a nose for quality, then the students will be all too aware of the gap between where they are and where they want to be. What they will not know is how best to move forward. Providing them with process criteria breaks the long journey into smaller steps from where the learners are to where they need to be, making it more manageable.

Learning intention:				
Criteria	**4**	**3**	**2**	**1**

Figure 2.8: Template for building a rubric from success criteria.

*Visit **go.SolutionTree.com/assessment** for a free reproducible version of this figure.*

Formative assessment expert and former teacher Shirley Clarke (2005) gives the following example of process criteria:

> Learning intention: to write an effective characterization
>
> Product success criterion: the reader will feel as if they know the person
>
> Process success criteria: the characterization includes at least two of the following:
>
> - the character's hobbies and interests
> - the character's attitudes toward self and others
> - examples of the character's extrovert or introvert personality
> - examples of the character's likes and dislikes (p. 31)

This example clearly shows how the process criteria break down the end goal, or success criteria, into small, manageable, and measurable steps. Writing frames are, likewise, examples of process criteria, because they structure the student's response. However, in the same way that leg braces are useful to individuals with weak legs but may feel like an awkward constraint for those who are healthy, writing frames can help some students but will prevent others from responding creatively. We need to realize that process criteria are, at the same time, both constraints *and* affordances for our students, and so we need to be thoughtful about how we frame them and how we use them.

Using the template in figure 2.9 (page 28), fill in your learning intention and a success criterion from the previous exercises. Then, create process criteria that will aid your students in meeting the success criterion. You may have to be selective about the criterion you choose. Not all will require a process. Discuss your process criteria with colleagues and identify any commonalities you find in which tasks or situations would best lend themselves to working with process criteria.

Learning intention:	
Success criterion:	
Process criteria	1.
	2.
	3.
	4.
	5.

Figure 2.9: Template for creating process criteria.

*Visit **go.SolutionTree.com/assessment** for a free reproducible version of this figure.*

Sample Student Work

While rubrics and process criteria certainly have their place in the classroom, the best way to help students understand what success criteria look like is to have students look at examples of other students' work and to engage in a discussion about each paper's strengths and weaknesses. This really gets to the heart of *how* to meet the learning goal. Rubrics tell us in words, but sample work shows us in practice.

For example, an elementary school teacher is teaching her class how to write book reports. Before she asks students to write their own reports, she chooses five examples from one of last year's classes, and groups of students have to decide whether some of these are better than others. If the groups decide that some are, indeed, better than others (as they always do!), they rank the pieces of work in terms of their quality, and then each group reports back in a whole-class session. Once each group shares its responses, the teacher invites students to give reasons for their views, and these are then used to co-construct a scoring rubric for book reports. As noted earlier, this is not a democratic process. The teacher uses her own subject-matter knowledge to shape the discussion, thus ensuring that the scoring rubric faithfully captures developing notions of competence in the subject.

> As many teachers have discovered, students are much better at spotting errors and weaknesses in the work of others than they are in their own. Once students have pointed out such errors or weaknesses, they are more likely to avoid repeating them in their own work. (Wiliam, 2018, p. 77)

One way of drawing together a session in which the class determines weaknesses in other students' work is to compile a list of *what not to write* in which students share pitfalls that they recommend others avoid. Use figure 2.10 as a template. However, be sure to always keep the student work anonymous, and do not provide the work of a current student. As we are highlighting errors or weaknesses, anonymity can both protect students and allow students to provide more criticism of the piece. Consent is not necessary, though if the student is still in the building, it certainly would be appropriate to ask!

Sample student work:		
What Not to Write	**Reason**	**Rewrite**

Figure 2.10: *What Not to Write* template.

*Visit **go.SolutionTree.com/assessment** for a free reproducible version of this figure.*

It can also be useful to use student examples to exemplify excellent work. For example, a high school teacher gives his class the task of writing a paper. The teacher gathers the papers and assigns each paper a provisional grade in his gradebook but does not write anything on the papers. The following day, students receive their own essays, together with copies of what the teacher judges to be three exemplary essays (either from past classes or a different class), which the teacher asks them to read before the next lesson. During the next lesson, the class discusses what it thinks are the notable features of the three essays judged as good. The teacher then invites all students to redraft and resubmit their essays. Two particular features of this technique are worth noting. First, it exemplifies outstanding work in a concrete way. Second, and probably more important, the students have to do intellectual work to compare their own work with the examples the teacher provides, so the feedback is more engaging than it would be had the students been given feedback that someone else provided.

Students are able to intellectually engage with the idea of quality work at a very young age. For example, a kindergarten class is using watercolor paint, and after about fifteen minutes, the teacher holds up one girl's painting and asks the class to suggest why the teacher thinks this is a particularly good example. A boy looks at the painting that is being held up and looks at his own painting, and after some moments, he says, "Because it's not all brown." The boy realizes that he has been too impatient in his painting and has not waited for the paint to dry before using a different color. The next time he paints, the boy will be able to recall his conclusions and improve his own painting, despite his early age.

> When a single example of the highest quality work is shown to students, this example may be seen as a model to be copied. . . . Students [should] see that there [is] not a single "royal road" to success, but in fact many ways of getting an A. (Wiliam, 2018, p. 76)

Choose-swap-choose is another technique for engaging students at an early age. The teacher asks each student in the class to write the letter *D* ten times. Each student then chooses which of his or her ten Ds he or she thinks is the best and circles it. The students then swap with a neighbor, and the neighbor circles which of his or her peer's Ds he or she thinks is the best. If the neighbors disagree, they discuss why. The opportunities for students to talk about quality work are practically unlimited.

Take a moment and consider a current or upcoming learning intention for your class. What examples of student work can you share to help illustrate these success criteria? Fill out figure 2.11 to make a plan for using this technique in your classroom.

Exit Passes

To find out what the students have learned, the best way is to simply ask them. One way to do this is with exit passes. With younger students, teachers may find the acronym WALT (We Are Learning To . . .), introduced by Shirley Clarke (2001), to be useful. Teachers can also supplement with TIB (This Is Because . . .; Clarke, 2001) to help students see how a particular learning intention fits in with other things they have done. Reproduce figure 2.12 to use as exit passes for your students. Go through the exit passes before the next day so you can alter your instruction as necessary to ensure students are on the right track.

Have older students (fourth grade and up) design test items, with correct answers, about their learning. This technique is particularly useful both for getting students to clarify, share, and understand learning intentions and for informing the teacher about the students' level of understanding. In this way, the teacher can find out what students think they have been learning. This is often different from what the teacher *thinks* they have been learning, as what the teacher thinks the students have been learning is irrelevant!

Context of Learning

One last item of note: we must also consider the context of learning when sharing and clarifying learning intentions and success criteria. If we only test students on the things we have taught them, they are, of course, likely to do well, but so what? Clarke (2005) points out that this kind of shallow approach to teaching and assessment is often the result of confusion between the learning intention and the context of learning. As teachers, we are not interested in our students' ability to do what we have taught them to do. Rather, we are only interested in their ability to apply their newly acquired knowledge to a similar but different context.

Clarke (2005) gives the following example. A middle school teacher has been teaching a unit on food production in the developing world. She tells the class that the learning intention is to understand the impact of

Class: Lesson:	Learning intention: Success criteria:

Sample student work:
What the example is meant to show:
 	
   •
 	
   •
 	
   •
 	
How students will demonstrate their understanding:

Sample student work:
What the example is meant to show:
 	
   •
 	
   •
 	
   •
 	
How students will demonstrate their understanding:

Sample student work:
What the example is meant to show:
 	
   •
 	
   •
 	
   •
 	
How students will demonstrate their understanding:

Figure 2.11: Plan for using student work to share success criteria.

*Visit **go.SolutionTree.com/assessment** for a free reproducible version of this figure.*

We are learning to . . .   This is because . . .

Figure 2.12: Exit pass template for learning intentions.

*Visit **go.SolutionTree.com/assessment** for a free reproducible version of this figure.*

banana production on the banana producers. The students study this topic, and at the end of the unit, the teacher conducts an assessment in which he or she requires students to show what they have learned about the impact of banana production on banana producers. Since they have been spending an hour a day on this topic, most students are able to get high scores on the assessment. But what exactly have they learned? A far better learning intention would be to understand the impact of production on producers in the developing world with banana production serving only as the context of the learning. The success criterion—how the teacher finds out whether the learning intention has been satisfied—could then be whether the students can transfer what they learned about banana production to, say, sugar production.

Table 2.1 draws on Clarke's (2005) work to provide some examples in which the teacher has confused the learning intention with the context of the learning and to present ways in which the teacher might reframe the learning objective.

Table 2.1: Examples of Confused and Clarified Learning Intentions

Context of Learning	Confused Learning Intention	Clarified Learning Intention
Changing a bicycle tire	To be able to write instructions on how to change a bicycle tire	To be able to write clear instructions
Discussing assisted suicide	To be able to present an argument for or against assisted suicide	To be able to present arguments either for or against emotionally charged propositions
Consulting the local priest	To know what the local priest does	To know the duties and responsibilities of religious leaders
Discovering movie-going habits	To produce and analyze a questionnaire about movie-going habits	To construct and analyze questionnaire data
Learning the preferred habitat of pill bugs	To design an experiment to find out what conditions pill bugs prefer	To design fair tests for scientific questions

Source: Clarke, 2005.

Another benefit of separating the learning intention from the context of the learning is that it is much easier to differentiate instruction without creating a classroom in which different students are working toward different goals. All students can be working toward the same learning intention; the differentiation comes, instead, in the success criteria. One effective way to do this is to differentiate the success criteria by how far students are able to transfer their learning to novel contexts. All students should be able to transfer what they have learned to similar contexts, while others can show how far they can transfer what they have learned.

In Your Classroom

It's very easy to read about a technique, get excited about its use in your classroom, and then get swept up in the day to day of teaching and never find time to incorporate it. That is why we strongly recommend that you make a concrete plan at the end of each strategy to incorporate just one technique from the chapter in your instruction. We will provide you with a planning template (see figure 2.13); now it's up to you to try it out. Once you have given it a good chance, reflect on how well it worked, and note any modifications that make sense for your classroom.

Strategy: Clarifying, Sharing, and Understanding Learning Intentions and Success Criteria
Lesson:
Technique:
Expectations and goals for using this technique:
Results:
Modifications for future use:

Figure 2.13: Plan for clarifying, sharing, and understanding learning intentions and success criteria.

*Visit **go.SolutionTree.com/assessment** for a free reproducible version of this figure.*

It seems obvious that to get anywhere, it helps to be clear about where you are going; however, sharing learning intentions and success criteria with students has not traditionally been regarded as important. Like everything else in teaching, there are no simple rules, and it is up to the teacher to exercise his or her professional judgment in how best to communicate learning intentions and success criteria to students. There are many sources of advice for teachers about the construction of learning intentions and success criteria, but developing good learning intentions is more craft than science and will always depend on teachers' creativity.

Once teachers and students are clear about where they are headed, the next step, of course, is to understand whether they are on track. For that, it is necessary to collect evidence about where students are in their learning, which is the subject of the next chapter.

Discussion Questions

You may answer the following questions independently or with your team to reinforce the chapter's key points.

1. Where do you get your learning intentions, and how do you determine these success criteria?

2. How do you know if your students truly understand the learning intention and how to meet these success criteria?

3. How does the context affect learning? And what can you do to ensure that the learning transfers to other contexts?

4. What technique from this chapter would you like to try, and why does it make sense for your students?

Chapter 3

Eliciting Evidence of Learners' Achievement

We discovered in the previous chapter the importance of being clear about what we want students to learn. Once we've accomplished that, we need to ascertain where the students are in meeting that learning goal. In many classrooms, the process of eliciting such evidence is done mainly on the fly—teachers almost always plan the instructional activities in which they will engage their students, but they rarely plan in detail how they are going to find out where the students are in their learning. This chapter emphasizes the importance of planning the assessment process and provides guidelines on how to obtain evidence of student learning through a high-engagement classroom and high-quality questioning. The chapter also offers some practical guidance on how to use questions effectively to adjust instruction to meet students' needs.

Current Practice

As we did in the previous chapter, let's take a moment to review our current practices for eliciting evidence of student learning. Use figure 3.1 (page 38) to note all relevant practices and how well you believe they work in your classroom. The third column is for any additional notes you may have, such as "This practice works very well when students are in small groups."

If you are working with a colleague or team, share your current practices and discuss their effectiveness in your classrooms. You may find, as you share practices with others, that the outcomes are different. This is a great opportunity to get tips and ideas from your colleagues.

The High-Engagement Classroom

When we, as teachers, ask students a question and get the answer we were hoping for, we tend to conclude that the students' learning is heading in the right direction. However, in relying on this method alone, there is a real danger in assuming our students' learning is on track when it is, in fact, heading off in a completely

Practice for Eliciting Achievement Evidence	Effectiveness	Notes

Figure 3.1: Inventory of current practices for the strategy of eliciting evidence of learners' achievement.

*Visit **go.SolutionTree.com/assessment** for a free reproducible version of this figure.*

different direction. Students may give an answer for a reason that you hadn't even thought of. Or perhaps we get only one answer—from the student with his or her hand raised—and assume the other students have the same answer in their heads.

We believe there are only two good reasons to ask questions in class: (1) to cause thinking and (2) to provide information for the teacher about what to do next. In almost any classroom, some students nearly dislocate their shoulders in their eagerness to raise their hand and show the teacher that they have an answer to the question that the teacher has just asked. In the same classroom, however, other students stay below the radar and avoid being called on. We need to create a classroom environment in which participation is not optional. This isn't to be cruel, although to some students it may seem that way. Rather, it is to ensure we know where every student is in his or her learning—and we cannot know this without the student's participation.

> When a teacher is having a discussion with one particular student, it is not enough that other students are quiet. If we want to create a community of learners, then it is important that when one student is speaking, the other students are listening appreciatively to what that student and teacher are saying. (Wiliam, 2018, p. 99)

High-engagement classrooms appear to have a significant impact on student achievement. In one study, fourth-grade classrooms followed the Thinking Together program (Dawes, Mercer, & Wegerif, 2000), a program that provided teachers with twelve lesson plans to help students develop their ability to use language as a tool for thinking about science and mathematics, both individually and in collaboration with other students. These students outperformed controls in similar schools on both teacher-constructed measures and standardized science achievement tests (Mercer, Dawes, Wegerif, & Sams, 2004). More surprisingly, these students outperformed controls on Raven's Progressive Matrices, a purely spatial test of intelligence. Engaging in classroom discussion—using language as a tool—really does make you smarter.

We will now discuss three techniques useful to creating a high-engagement classroom environment.

1. No hands up

2. Wait time

3. All-student response systems

No Hands Up

When teachers allow students to choose whether to participate or not—for example, by allowing them to raise their hands to show they have an answer—they are actually making the achievement gap worse. This is because those who are participating are getting smarter, while those avoiding engagement are forgoing the opportunities to increase their ability (Black, Harrison, Lee, Marshall, & Wiliam, 2004).

This is why many teachers now employ a rule of "no hands up, except to ask a question" in their classrooms (Leahy et al., 2005). The teacher poses a question and then picks a student at random to answer. Alternatively, the teacher poses a question, allows a moment for students to discuss with their neighbors, and then picks a student at random to answer. One middle school teacher describes this technique as *pose-pause-pounce-bounce* (Wiliam, 2018). In it, she:

- Poses the question

- Pauses for at least five seconds (Sometimes, to help her measure the time, she mutters, under her breath, "One, two, three, four, got to wait a little more.")

- Pounces on one student at random for the answer
- Bounces that student's answer to another student, again at random, saying, "What do you think of that answer?"

> Like any technique in teaching, educators should apply random questioning with sensitivity and discretion. Many students are very shy . . . , and teachers need to be sensitive to this. However, deciding . . . never to call on that student may be just as bad, since that would allow the student not to engage in any of what is going on. (Wiliam, 2018, p. 94)

Some teachers may claim to be able to choose students at random without any help, but most realize that when they are in a hurry to wrap up a discussion so that the class can move on, they often draw on one of the usual suspects for a good answer. This is why many teachers find that using some randomization device is useful (Wiliam, 2018). Examples of these can be downloaded from the Internet, and randomization routines are often included in the software for interactive whiteboards. There are now even apps for the iPhone into which teachers can enter names and the app will draw a name at random. However, a beaker of Popsicle sticks on which the students' names are written does the job just as well. Popsicle sticks are also much more flexible; one teacher has punished inattentive students by writing their name on ten additional sticks and adding them to the beaker. Many teachers give the beaker to a student to pull the selection for the day in order to resolve any concern that teachers are rigging the choice.

The major advantage of Popsicle sticks, however, can also be a disadvantage. It is essential to replace the sticks to ensure that students who have recently answered know they need to stay on task, but then the teacher cannot guarantee that all students will be called on to answer. One way around this is to leave the selected sticks out of the beaker but then replace them when students who have already answered a question seem off task. Another option is to have a dividing screen in the beaker, and when teachers select sticks, they place the selection in the "discards" side of the beaker. That way, if students who have just answered a question seem off task, the teacher can select a stick from the discards side to reinforce the idea that just because one answers a question does not mean one can relax for the next several questions.

This isn't an easy change by any means. The traditional classroom allows students to show the teacher they know the answer when they choose to. Having this control is very important to many students. Students who do not typically engage in classroom discussion will need time to adapt to this practice and feel comfortable sharing their answers with classmates, whether those answers are right or wrong. Students who do typically engage in classroom discussion are used to being the discussion leaders, and it can be part of their self-identity. Not having the opportunity to show what they know can be discouraging. Watch *The Classroom Experiment* (Barry & Hardy, 2010; http://bit.ly/2txwC8z) to see the *no hands up* technique in action. (Visit **go.SolutionTree.com/assessment** to access live links to the websites mentioned in this book.) Then, record your observations in figure 3.2.

Now that you've seen *no hands up* in action, let's give it a try in your own classroom. As you likely noted, this isn't a quick-fix exercise; it requires a new classroom contract. The intention here is twofold. Not only do we want to elicit evidence of learning from students participating in class, but we also want to create an environment in which we measure success not in right or wrong answers, but in making mistakes, talking through possibilities, and learning. Commit to trying this technique in your classroom for three weeks, and track your progress in figure 3.3 (page 42).

What is Dylan Wiliam's advice to teachers about *no hands up*?	
What were the advantages of *no hands up* in the classroom?	
What were the disadvantages of *no hands up* in the classroom?	
Do you think this technique will work in your classroom? Explain why or why not.	
What would you do differently to customize this technique for your classroom?	

Figure 3.2: Observations on the *no hands up* technique.

*Visit **go.SolutionTree.com/assessment** for a free reproducible version of this figure.*

Technique: *No Hands Up*		
Date	**Successful (+) or Unsuccessful (–)**	**Notes and Observations**
Summary of *no hands up* technique:		

Figure 3.3: Observations on the *no hands up* technique in your classroom.

*Visit **go.SolutionTree.com/assessment** for a free reproducible version of this figure.*

It is important to note, both for your own information and when implementing your new classroom contract with students, that you are not using *no hands up* as a *gotcha* to embarrass students; rather, you're using it to ensure that all students realize that participation is not optional. There are a couple of techniques you may like to use to minimize the shock of the gotcha effect on students when implementing *no hands up*. First, students are much less likely to be tongue-tied if they have been given a few minutes to think about the answer to the question and to discuss it with a neighbor before the teacher chooses a student to respond. Requiring students to talk to a neighbor has two advantages. First, it allows students to assemble their thoughts, which provides an opportunity for students to rehearse the vocabulary that they might use in a response. Second, teachers can ask the student they select at random to report his or her partner's answer from the partner talk, which lowers the stakes with *no hands up*. This is less emotionally charged, because students are relaying what someone else has said instead of their own thoughts, and, of course, it has the additional advantage of making students listen to each other.

> Practices that support the students without letting them off the hook are allowing students to *phone a friend*, or for multiple-choice items, they can *ask the audience* or ask to go *fifty-fifty*, where the teacher removes two incorrect responses. Even when the student resists answering a question, the teacher looks for ways to maintain the student's engagement. (Wiliam, 2018, p. 96)

Another concern when moving to random selection in your classroom is that, as mentioned earlier, the technique will likely be unpopular with students who participate regularly. For some, this is because they are no longer able to show the teacher that they have the answer. One way to tackle this issue is to ask two students at random for responses to a question, and then ask the remainder of the class if anyone has anything else to contribute. It is also essential to ask the question first, give students time to think and perhaps talk with a neighbor, and then pick the student to answer. Doing it the other way around guarantees that all but the selected student know they do not need to pay attention.

Wait Time

People do not generally like silence during discussions. It makes us uncomfortable, and often it is our human nature to rush to fill that quiet. Add to that the pressure teachers are under to get through lessons as quickly and efficiently as possible, and it's no wonder that teachers provide very little wait time after asking students questions.

However, how much time a teacher allows a student to respond—the teacher's *wait time*—is important. Teachers do not allow students much time to answer questions (see, for example, Fredericks, 2005; Rowe, 1974), and if they do not receive a response quickly, they will often provide a clue to "help" the student, weaken the question in some way, or move on to another student. But when the question requires thought, increasing the time following a teacher's question from the average wait time of less than a second to just three seconds causes measurable increases in learning, although the benefits are lost if the wait time is increased beyond three seconds as the lessons lose pace (Tobin, 1987).

Because this technique adds so much to student engagement, we should give it a shot in our classrooms. Increasing your post-question wait time to three seconds sounds a lot simpler than it actually is, so start slowly, and let the students know ahead of time about the change (see figure 3.4, page 45).

Also keep in mind the amount of time between the student's answer and the teacher's evaluation of that answer—what we might call *elaboration time*. This is just as, if not more, important than extending wait time because when the teacher does not evaluate the students' responses immediately, then students are likely to extend their responses, and when they are talking, they are thinking, and when they are thinking, they are learning.

All-Student Response Systems

The idea of an *all-student response system* is very simple: the teacher asks a question in a way that allows him or her to get a response from every student in real time. Because teachers require input from students on whether they are ready to move on from the topic or whether more time needs to be devoted to ensure learning, teachers must be able to get a response from every single student. Some teachers employ class polls—going around the class and asking each student for his or her view on a question—but these work well only when every student expresses a view, and getting around the whole class can cause a considerable loss of momentum. It is best to collect the information from every student at the same time. There are four all-student response systems you may wish to try in your classroom: (1) self-reports, (2) ABCD cards, (3) mini whiteboards, and (4) exit passes.

Self-Reports

Many teachers collect information from the whole class simultaneously with techniques like *thinking thumbs* or *fist to five*, where students indicate their understanding either through the positioning of the thumb (pointing up: confident; horizontally: not sure; down: still confused) or with a number from zero to five by holding up a clenched fist (zero: do not understand at all) or the appropriate number of fingers (up to five fingers: confident). The problem with such techniques is that they are self-reports, and, as we know from experience, self-reports are unreliable.

However, a very small change can transform useless self-reports into a powerful tool. Simply make sure that the question the teacher is asking is cognitive rather than affective—in other words, that the question asks about thinking, not a feeling. For example, an elementary school teacher was teaching her students when the word *its* needed an apostrophe and when it didn't (Wiliam, 2018). On the board, she wrote the sentence, "Its on its way" and invited students to come to the board and add any necessary punctuation. One student came up and added a period; a second added an apostrophe to the first *its*; and a third student added an apostrophe to the second *its*. The teacher then asked, "Is that now correct?" and every student had to respond by holding out his or her thumb pointing up or down. Just this small change in the way the question is posed creates a situation in which no student slips through the crack of avoiding participation. If the students signal that it is correct when it is not, then they reveal that they do not understand. On the other hand, if they signal that it is incorrect, then the teacher may ask them to go to the front of the class to correct the error.

Review an upcoming lesson plan, and write down five self-report questions you would typically ask the class in figure 3.5 (page 46). Do any of these questions ask the students to report to you on how confident they feel about the material, whether they understand it or not? If so, rework the question into one that allows the students to show you whether they truly know the content. Should you have difficulty with this exercise, partner with a colleague and share the work.

Technique: *Wait Time*		
Date	**Successful (+) or Unsuccessful (−)**	**Notes and Observations**
Summary of *wait time* technique:		

Figure 3.4: Observations on the *wait time* technique in your classroom.

*Visit **go.SolutionTree.com/assessment** for a free reproducible version of this figure.*

Self-Report Question	Rewritten Question

Figure 3.5: Reflection on self-reports.

*Visit **go.SolutionTree.com/assessment** for a free reproducible version of this figure.*

The problem with using fingers and thumbs for self-reporting is that they work best with questions that require a single response (a drawback of most electronic clickers, too). That is why many teachers adopt ABCD cards.

ABCD Cards

For the ABCD cards technique, each student has a number of cards, and each card bears a single letter. Some teachers just use A, B, C, and D, while others use nine cards: A, B, C, D, E, F, G, H, and T (for true-or-false questions). Teachers and students can use these cards just like fingers, but they can also use them with questions for which there is more than one correct answer. Teachers also use ABCD cards when there are no right or wrong answers, but, instead, different views or opinions.

One elementary school teacher took the idea of cards one step further with what she called *letter corners* (Wiliam, 2018). She used multiple-choice questions with four options (A, B, C, and D). If each option had at least three students supporting it, she sent the students to the four corners of the room, which she labeled A, B, C, and D. The students' task in each corner was to work out how to convince the students in the other corners that their choice was the best. Occasionally, students sneaked from one corner to another. They moved surreptitiously because they worried that the teacher would think that they were cheating. However, of course, the teacher celebrated such changes of mind as indicating that the students learned something through discussion with peers.

A major difficulty with ABCD cards is that they generally require teachers to plan questions carefully ahead of time, and so they are less useful for spontaneous discussion. This is where mini whiteboards come in.

> The use of multiple correct answers allows the teacher to incorporate items that support differentiation, by including some responses that all students should be able to identify correctly but others that only the ablest students will be able to answer correctly. Such differentiation also helps keep the highest-achieving students challenged and, therefore, engaged. (Wiliam, 2018, p. 106)

Mini Whiteboards

The mini whiteboard isn't a modern invention; it is really just the latest reincarnation of the slates used in 19th century classrooms. Whiteboards are powerful tools in that the teacher can quickly frame a question and get an answer from the whole class, whether through asking elementary school students to write down a four-letter word with a short *i* sound or through asking students in an AP calculus class to sketch the graph of an equation.

Some teachers, whose schools lack the budget or interest in investing in mini whiteboards, have engineered cheaper alternatives to this technique. One teacher (Wiliam, 2018) wanted to use whiteboards, but the school's budget lacked sufficient money to acquire them, so, instead, she placed sheets of letter-sized white card stock inside page protectors to provide a low-cost alternative. Students then wrote on the page protectors with erasable markers. She realized that this was actually a far more flexible option than the mini whiteboards, because she was able to preprint different images on the inserts for specific lessons. When she was teaching mathematics, the insert could be a sheet of graph paper, and when she was teaching geography, it could be a map of the United States. No matter the insert, she was able to quickly and easily gather information from her class with little difficulty.

When using mini whiteboards, consider ahead of time the answer to the question you will be asking. You will be scanning the classroom to check the answer's accuracy; therefore, it is most efficient when the answer is three or fewer words. When questions require longer responses, teachers can use exit passes.

Exit Passes

Exit pass questions work best when there is a natural break in the instruction, such as a lunch break or the end of the class period; the teacher then has time to read through the students' responses and decide what to do next. Examples of exit pass questions include the following.

- Why can't you have a probability greater than 1?
- What is the difference between mass and weight?
- Why are historians concerned with bias when analyzing historical sources?
  (Wiliam, 2018, p. 108)

If students have written their names on the back, the teacher can use the exit passes as place settings for the next period with that class. The teacher can either create homogenous groups, so that he or she can work with the students who are having the greatest difficulty, or create heterogeneous groups in which there is at least one student who provided a good answer. Of course, since the work hasn't been formally graded, the students with the good answers don't know who they are, which leads to more open discussion.

Exit passes can also be used to bridge two lessons. A middle school mathematics class was learning to solve equations with a single unknown, and five minutes before the end of the lesson, the teacher posted the following six questions and asked the students to work out the answers on an exit pass.

1. $3x + 3 = 12$
2. $5x - 1 = 19$
3. $12 - 2x = 3$

4. $4 = 28 - 3x$

5. $4x - 3 = 2x + 7$

6. $3 - 2x = 17 - 4x$

Four of the questions related to what the class had learned that lesson. The last two questions related to what she planned to do for the following lesson, where the unknown quantity appeared on both sides of the equation. The teacher was pleased to see that most of the students answered the first four correctly. However, few students answered either of the last two questions correctly, so she could see that what she had planned to do for the next lesson was, in fact, appropriate.

High-Quality Questioning

Probably the most common instructional decision teachers make every day is, "Do I need to go over this one more time, or is it OK to move on?" In most classrooms, teachers generate the evidence for this decision by making up a question on the spur of the moment, asking the class, and selecting one of the students who raises his or her hand to answer. If that student answers correctly, the teacher generally says, "Good," and moves on. Asking a random student rather than a volunteer is better, but the real problem is that the teacher is basing the class's readiness on one or two students' performances. Teachers need to use all-student response systems routinely if they are to harness the power of high-quality questioning to inform their instructional decisions.

The techniques in this section—multiple-choice questions, questions as statements, and question shells—create student engagement while providing the teacher with evidence about the extent of each student's learning so that the teacher is able to adjust the instruction to better meet the students' learning needs. Of course, the evidence's quality—and, therefore, the instructional adjustments' quality—depends on the quality of the questions the teacher asks.

Teachers must acknowledge that what their students learn is not necessarily what they intend, and this is inevitable because of teaching's unpredictability. Thus, it is essential that teachers explore students' thinking before assuming that students understand something. However, obtaining these powerful insights into students' thinking is far from straightforward.

> Questions that provide a window into students' thinking are not easy to generate, but they are crucially important if we are to improve the quality of students' learning. (Wiliam, 2018, p. 89)

Often, such questions seem unfair. Many mathematics teachers' reaction to the following question, taken from the Chelsea Diagnostic Mathematics Tests for algebra (Hart, Brown, Kerslake, Küchemann, & Ruddock, 1985), illustrates this point:

Simplify (if possible) $2a + 5b$

As well as teachers, students perceive the question as unfair because they assume that in answering test questions, they should have to do some work. Thus, they contend, it must be possible to simplify this expression, otherwise, the teacher wouldn't have asked the question—after all, you don't get points in a test for doing nothing. But, of course, the answer to this question—testing the students' knowledge of algebra—is that it *cannot* be simplified further. Such a question may fall short of standards and fairness guidelines established for items in a high-stakes test (for example, Educational Testing Service, 2002). But for finding out whether or not students understand a key principle in algebra, it is a useful question. If a student can be tempted to simplify $2a + 5b$, then the teacher should want to know that, because addressing this misunderstanding will be essential before the student can make progress.

In general, it is better to assume that students do not know something when they do than it is to assume they do know something when they actually don't. What makes a question useful, therefore, is that it must be very unlikely that the student will get the correct answer for the wrong reason. In addition, teachers need to check for understanding quickly. Therefore, it should take no longer than two minutes, and ideally less than one minute, for all students to respond to a question, and it must be possible for the teacher to view and interpret the responses from the class in thirty seconds (preferably fewer). The teacher risks students getting off task and displaying disruptive behavior if he or she takes any longer than this to make sense of the students' responses. So, with those requirements in place, what qualities are key to developing high-quality questions?

The first quality of high-quality questions is that students with the right idea about whatever it is we want them to know, understand, or be able to do should get different answers than students who do not have the right idea. Ideally, it would be impossible for students to get the right answer for the wrong reason. One way to ensure such questions is to involve groups of teachers. One group of teachers develops a question, which it then hands to a second group of teachers to identify a way in which a student might get the correct answer with incorrect reasoning. If the group can, then it hands the question back to the first group to refine. Such teacher collaboration will help to build a stock of good questions.

Let's try this out. Write down two questions in figure 3.6 (page 50) that you believe give you a good understanding of what your students know (preferably from an upcoming lesson), and put them to the test with a colleague or team. Your colleague's task is to work the problem in every way he or she can imagine a student doing to see if it's possible to accidentally get the right answer. If you are working alone, we highly encourage you to pull in a colleague for this particular exercise, as an outside view is necessary to get as many solutions as possible.

The second quality of high-quality questions is to assist instructional decision making quickly; the answers should be *interpretable*. That is, if students choose a particular incorrect response, the teacher knows (or at least has a pretty good idea) why they have done so. A multiple-choice question in which the incorrect responses relate to well-known naïve conceptions, such as the following question on Spanish pronouns a group of Spanish teachers from Chico Unified School District, California, developed (figure 3.7, page 50).

Anyone who has taught Spanish to native English speakers knows that they have two particular difficulties in learning about pronouns: (1) which pronoun to choose and (2) where it should go. This item is clever because in one of the responses, the correct pronoun is in the wrong place; in another, the placement is correct, but the pronoun is incorrect; and in others, there are multiple errors. This question took quite a while to generate—certainly much more time than teachers would normally take to write a single question—but it will still be a good question in twenty years' time, because native English speakers will have the same difficulty with pronoun selection and placement when learning Spanish.

Knowing why students choose a particular answer means you can use those answers to make changes (or not) to your instruction to meet your students' needs. This may mean staying the course with your instruction or creating small groups to help students who answer incorrectly with the same answer. High-quality questions do not simply look for the right answer; rather, they are strategic with their incorrect answers as well.

Question	Solution (Show Your Work!)

Figure 3.6: Template to test questions for quality.

Visit **go.SolutionTree.com/assessment** *for a free reproducible version of this figure.*

Which of the following is the correct translation for "I give the book to him"?

    a. Yo lo doy el libro.

    b. Yo doy le el libro.

    c. Yo le doy el libro.

    d. Yo doy lo el libro.

    e. Yo doy el libro le.

    f. Yo doy el libro lo.

Source: Wiliam, 2018.

Figure 3.7: Example of a diagnostic question in Spanish.

When teachers listen to student responses, many focus more on the correctness of the answers than what they can learn about the student's understanding (Even & Tirosh, 1995; Haug & Ødegaard, 2015; Heid, Blume, Zbiek, & Edwards, 1999). It is easy to identify such teachers because when they get incorrect answers from students, they respond with things like, "Almost," "Close," or "Nearly; try again." What the teacher really means is, "Give me the correct answer so that I can get on with the rest of my script for the lesson." Brent Davis (1997) calls such behavior *evaluative listening*.

As Wiliam (2018) states, "Teachers who listen evaluatively to their students' answers learn only whether their students know what they want them to know" (p. 98). If the students cannot answer correctly, then the teachers learn only that the students didn't get it and that they need to reteach the material—only, presumably, better. However, when teachers realize that there is often information about *how* to teach something better in what students say—and thus how to adjust their instruction to better meet students' needs—they listen *interpretively*. What such teachers seek to learn from the students' responses is not, "Did they get it?" but rather, "What can I learn about the students' thinking by attending to what they say?" The shift from evaluative to interpretive listening was perhaps most eloquently summarized by a girl in a seventh-grade classroom, who, when asked if she had noticed any change in her teacher over recent months, said, "When Miss used to ask a question, she used to be interested in the right answer. Now she's interested in what we think" (Hodgen & Wiliam, 2006, p. 16).

Psychologist David P. Ausubel (1968) argues that the most important factor influencing learning is what the learner already knows, and that the teacher's job is to ascertain this and to teach accordingly. Educators are better able to find out what their students know when they challenge students to think. To present questions that have more than one correct answer and problems that have no solution. To think beyond traditional lecture-style instruction and engage their students in critical thinking to answer the high-quality questions they ask.

The remainder of this section will discuss three techniques that you can adapt for formative, high-quality questioning: (1) multiple-choice questions, (2) questions as statements, and (3) question shells.

Multiple-Choice Questions

Some people argue that multiple-choice questions have no place in educational assessment (Wiliam, 2018). For instance, some criticize multiple-choice questions because these questions assess only lower-order-thinking skills such as factual recall or application of a standard algorithm (Pomeroy, 2014); although as the previous examples show, they can, if carefully designed, address higher-order-thinking skills. Another criticism of using multiple-choice questions in tests is that there is no opportunity for the student to negotiate the question's meaning with the question-setter or the machine that does the scoring.

However, there are good reasons for preferring the multiple-choice format for formative assessment purposes. In the classroom, multiple-choice questions have one great feature in their favor: they limit the number of possible student responses. When a teacher faces a sea of thirty whiteboards, for example, each with a different response, it can be bewildering. Using multiple-choice questions provides a means for sorting all the students' responses, so that precious classroom time is not spent trying to make sense of the students' answers.

> When designing multiple-choice questions for classroom use, . . . [try] to make it less likely that students get the right answer for the wrong reason. (Wiliam, 2018, p. 118)

For example, let's say a teacher asks her Spanish class the multiple-choice question from figure 3.7, tells the students to write their answers on their whiteboards, and has them show their answers simultaneously. With this one high-quality question, the teacher administers, grades, and puts herself in a position to take remedial action regarding a whole-class quiz in a matter of minutes, without giving herself a pile of grading to do. She does not have a grade for each student, but this is a small price to pay for such an agile piece of teaching. This is, in fact, a canonical example of formative assessment: the teacher requires every student in the class to indicate his or her understanding, which engages every student, and she uses the information to make on-the-spot adjustments to her instruction.

Questions as Statements

Asking questions may not always be the best way to generate good classroom discussions. If, instead, the teacher frames the question as a statement, such as, "Russia was most to blame for the outbreak of World War I," students seem to respond more thoughtfully because they realize that just agreeing or dissenting is not enough—they need to provide reasons. Teachers can usually enhance the quality of discussion further when they give students the opportunity to discuss their responses in pairs or small groups before responding (a technique often called *think-pair-share*).

In figure 3.8, write down three statements that can start a class discussion for an upcoming lesson. After you try them out in the classroom, note whether they are effective in generating the learning you hope for and why or why not.

Statement	Effectiveness		
	Was the statement effective? Why or why not?	Yes	No
	Was the statement effective? Why or why not?	Yes	No
	Was the statement effective? Why or why not?	Yes	No

Figure 3.8: Statements to promote discussion.

*Visit **go.SolutionTree.com/assessment** for a free reproducible version of this figure.*

For this technique to work, you must have a learning environment in which students are comfortable questioning the teacher. What we certainly don't want is to make a statement such as "Fish are mammals" and have students diligently write down this "fact" in their notebooks. To get started (and to break the traditional act of writing down everything the teacher says and taking it at face value), you may find that, at first, it is helpful to offer a statement and then ask students whether they agree or not and why. This gives the students permission to disagree, thus making such a situation more comfortable for them. You can then lead into the more complex task of stimulating discussion through questions as statements.

Question Shells

There are a number of general structures, or *question shells*, that can help frame questions in ways that are more likely to reveal students' thinking. Two are "Why is _____ an example

of _____?" and "Why is _____ not an example of _____?"
(For example, "Why is a bird not an example of an insect?") Similarly, rather than asking, "Is magnesium a metal?" teachers are likely to generate more thoughtful and reasoned responses when they ask, "Why is magnesium an example of a metal?" Figure 3.9 shows other examples.

Original	Reframed
Is a square a trapezoid?	Why is a square an example of a trapezoid?
Is carbon a metal?	Why is carbon not an example of metal?
Is *être* a regular verb?	Why is *être* an example of an irregular verb?
Is this a sentence or a clause?	Why is this a clause rather than a sentence?
Is slate a metamorphic rock?	Why is slate an example of metamorphic rock?
Is *The Merchant of Venice* a comedy [or a tragedy]?	Why is *The Merchant of Venice* an example of a comedy [or a tragedy]?
Is 23 prime?	Why is 23 prime?
Is photosynthesis an endothermic reaction?	Why is photosynthesis an example of an endothermic reaction?

Source: Wiliam, 2018.

Figure 3.9: Examples of the use of question shells.

Another technique is to present students with a contrast and then ask them to explain the contrast, as figure 3.10 shows.

Original	Reframed
What is a prime number?	Why is 17 prime and 15 not?
What was life under apartheid like?	How were the lives of black people and white people different under apartheid?
Is a bat a mammal?	Why is a bat a mammal and a penguin not?

Source: Wiliam, 2018.

Figure 3.10: Examples of questions reframed in terms of contrasts.

Now that you've read through several examples, it's your turn to reframe. This type of question ties in nicely with learning intentions, success criteria, and backward design. Write down several yes-or-no or short-answer questions in the first column of figure 3.11 (page 54) that you would typically use in a lesson. Before you reframe those questions, however, consider the learning goals for the lesson. It's all very well and good to ask students to explain why *Romeo and Juliet* is a tragedy, but it doesn't get you very far if the learning goal is to understand iambic pentameter and its use in literature. Using either the question shells or the contrast method, fill in the following figure with the end goal of addressing the learning intention.

A further benefit of focusing on high-quality questions is . . . their portability. Most teachers find worksheets or other teachers' lesson plans to be of limited usefulness. However, high-quality questions seem to work across different schools, districts, states, cultures, and even languages. Indeed, sharing high-quality questions may be the most significant thing we can do to improve the quality of student learning. (Wiliam, 2018, p. 121)

Original	Reframed

Figure 3.11: Questions reframed to meet learning intention.

*Visit **go.SolutionTree.com/assessment** for a free reproducible version of this figure.*

In Your Classroom

Now that you've completed this chapter, it's time to make a plan to implement this strategy in your classroom. As you were reading, did a particular technique strike you? Which do you think would work best with the students in your classroom? While you are certainly welcome to try as many techniques as you want, we encourage you to give at least one a legitimate chance for success. Use figure 3.12 to plan for the strategy.

Strategy: Eliciting Evidence of Learners' Achievement
Lesson:
Technique:
Expectations and goals for using this technique:
Results:
Modifications for future use:

Figure 3.12: Plan for eliciting evidence of learners' achievement.

Visit **go.SolutionTree.com/assessment** *for a free reproducible version of this figure.*

Within a typical classroom, there is clearly not enough time for the teacher to teach each student as an individual, but with careful planning and thoughtfully applying the techniques we present in this chapter, the teacher can make the classroom a much more engaging place for students—and one in which the teacher is able to make rapid and effective instructional adjustments to meet all students' learning needs. Once the teacher knows where learners are in their learning, he or she is in a position to provide feedback to the learners about what to do next—and this is the subject of the next chapter.

Discussion Questions

You may answer the following questions independently or with your team to reinforce the chapter's key points.

1. Describe the learning environment in your classroom. Is there anything you would like to change about it?

2. Watch *The Classroom Experiment* (Barry & Hardy, 2010; http://bit.ly/2txwC8z) to observe the *no hands up* technique. How well do you think the formative assessment techniques worked? What changes would you make to best meet your students' needs?

3. How do you currently come up with the questions you ask your students? How can you ensure they are high quality?

4. What technique from this chapter would you like to try, and why does it make sense for your students?

Chapter 4

Providing Feedback That Moves Learning Forward

I t seems obvious that feedback to students about their work should help them learn, but it turns out that providing effective feedback is far more difficult than it appears. There are different types of feedback. Feedback can be praise or reprimand. Feedback can take the form of detailed comments on a student's work. Some consider grades or scores feedback, since educators are providing students with a response to their work. And in other cases, feedback could be a combination of all these. However, much of the feedback that students get has little or no effect on their learning, and some kinds of feedback are actually counterproductive. This chapter offers guidance on how teachers can give their students feedback that moves learning forward. It will discuss how teachers can use engineering principles to test the efficacy of their feedback, typical student reactions to feedback, how feedback functions formatively, and principles of effective feedback.

Current Practice

Let's take a moment to review your current practices for providing feedback. Use figure 4.1 (page 58) to note all relevant practices and how well you believe they work in your classroom.

Feedback and the Engineering Test

As we discovered in *Embedded Formative Assessment* (Wiliam, 2018), students receiving constructive feedback learned twice as fast as students given scores—in other words, they learned in one week what the other students took two weeks to learn (Elawar & Corno, 1985). *Constructive feedback*, as this book defines it, includes specific comments on errors, suggestions to the students about how to improve, and at least one positive remark. Feedback has the power to improve classroom learning (Elawar & Corno, 1985; Wiggins, 2012).

When considering whether a feedback practice is constructive and, therefore, applicable to this formative assessment strategy, it is helpful to think of the practice in terms of engineering. The term *feedback* is actually borrowed from engineering. Although the term *feedback* has been around for well over a hundred years,

Practice	Effectiveness	Notes

Figure 4.1: Inventory of current practices for the strategy of providing feedback that moves learning forward.

*Visit **go.SolutionTree.com/assessment** for a free reproducible version of this figure.*

mathematician and philosopher Norbert Wiener (1948) brought it to widespread use. The important feature of feedback, as used in engineering, is that it forms part of a feedback *loop*. A classic example of a feedback loop is using a thermostat to regulate a room's temperature (figure 4.2).

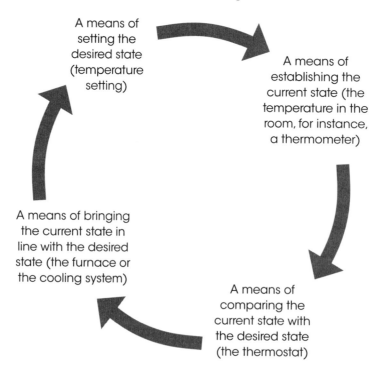

Figure 4.2: Feedback loop to regulate temperature.

For engineers, information about the discrepancy between the current and desired states is useless unless there is also a mechanism within the feedback loop to bring the current state closer to the desired state. In education, however, we use the term *feedback* for any information given to students about their current achievements. This practice sometimes misses the key quality of feedback in engineering—the need for a mechanism within the feedback loop to bring the student closer to the desired state of knowing what we want them to know. Just telling the students that their current performance falls short of where they need to be isn't what an engineer would recognize as feedback. If there is nothing connecting the thermostat to the furnace, then there is no feedback loop, and, therefore, no feedback.

Let's return now to your list of feedback practices in figure 4.1 and put each to the engineering test. In figure 4.3 (page 60), list those practices that you deemed effective in the previous exercise. Does the thermostat connect to the furnace? Label the feedback loop for each practice. If it doesn't meet the engineering test, think about what you could add to your practice to complete the loop. If you are working in a teacher team, share your results and add to your list any other practices that meet the engineering test.

Student Reactions to Feedback

Likely on your list of practices is giving both a grade (or score) and some kind of comment. This is probably the most prevalent form of feedback to students in North America (and, indeed, in most other countries; Wiliam, 2018). However, we've learned that even if teachers are providing careful diagnostic comments and then putting a score or a grade on the work, they are wasting their time (Wiliam, 2018). Students are interested in their grades, and that's pretty much it. Especially if there is no opportunity to improve on their initial efforts and possibly get a better score, students aren't going to bother reading comments. The high scorers already got their grade, and the low scorers are demotivated and don't want to read criticism. Teachers might as well just give a score or a grade—the students won't learn anything as a result, but teachers will save a great deal of time.

To provide feedback that will move learning forward, we must first understand students' relationship with feedback. We will explore what happens when students assess their performance relative to assessment goals, how students attribute success and failure, and the importance of praise.

Performance Relative to Goals

To try to understand why feedback could have such counterproductive—and unexpected—effects, Avraham N. Kluger and Angelo DeNisi (1996) look in detail at studies to determine when feedback does and does not improve performance. They discover that when the feedback draws attention to a gap between one's current performance and the goal, what happens depends on whether the current performance is higher or lower than the goal (Kluger & DeNisi, 1996).

When the feedback tells a student that he or she has already surpassed the goal, obviously one hopes that the student would seek to change the goal to one that is more demanding, but the student might instead take it as a signal to ease off and exert less effort. Also, the student may decide that the goal itself is worthless and abandon it entirely or reject the feedback as being irrelevant when success comes too easily.

Feedback Practice	Feedback Loop
	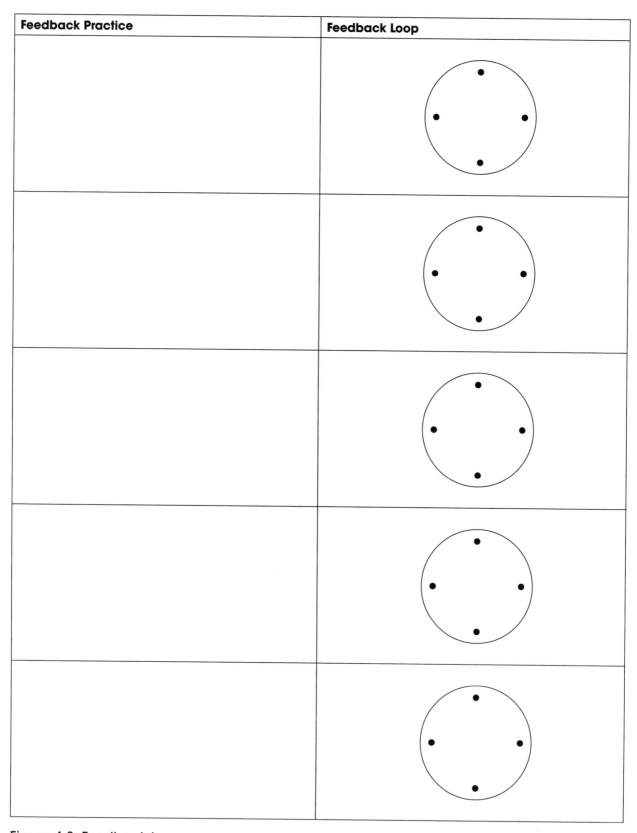

Figure 4.3: Feedback loops.

More commonly, a student may respond in the one of the following four ways when the feedback indicates that current performance falls short of the goal.

1. The student may change the goal. For example, a student may decide to settle for a B even though an A might be within her grasp when she feels it's too much work or too risky in terms of her self-image to attempt.

2. The student may abandon the goal altogether, as seen in the *learned helplessness* (Dweck, 1975) of students who face repeated indications that they are falling short. They decide that something is forever beyond them—for example, when a student says, "I'm no good at math."

3. The student may reject the feedback. This is quite common in workplace settings when, for example, someone who feels he contributes well beyond what was expected gets a neutral evaluation from a supervisor. Rejecting such feedback leads the worker to lower his commitment (and therefore, possibly, to reduce his performance).

4. The student may change behavior so as to increase performance to match the goal, which is presumably the response the person giving feedback intends.

We have seen that in almost two out of every five carefully designed scientific studies, information given to people about their performance lowers their subsequent performance (Kluger & DeNisi, 1996). When we give students feedback, eight things can happen, and six of them are bad. Table 4.1 summarizes these responses to feedback.

Table 4.1: Possible Responses to Feedback

Response Type	Feedback Indicates Performance Exceeds Goal	Feedback Indicates Performance Falls Short of Goal
Change Behavior	Exert less effort	*Increase effort*
Change Goal	*Increase aspiration*	Reduce aspiration
Abandon Goal	Decide goal is too easy	Decide goal is too hard
Reject Feedback	Ignore feedback	Ignore feedback

Only the two italicized kinds of responses are likely to improve performance. The other six, at best, do nothing and, at worst, lower performance, sometimes by a considerable degree.

The research also shows that it is very difficult, if not impossible, to predict which of these responses will occur (Kluger & DeNisi, 1996). It will depend on the individual receiving the feedback, the kind of task on which an educator gives feedback, and how the recipient perceives the person giving the feedback. One way to combat these difficulties in providing feedback is to promote a growth mindset.

Growth Mindset and Fixed Mindset

In a series of research studies spanning over thirty years, professor of psychology Carol S. Dweck and her colleagues investigate, among other things, how students make sense of their successes and failures. A result of this research is Dweck's (2006) focus on the underlying beliefs that students have about learning—namely, whether one's intelligence is fixed and there isn't anything he or she can do to change it (fixed mindset) or whether it is able to grow and change with one's effort (growth mindset).

Students who believe in *fixed* ability will see any assignment as a chance either to reaffirm their ability or to be shown up (Dweck, 2006). If they are confident in their ability to achieve the teacher's task for them, then they will attempt the task. However, if their confidence in their ability is low, then they may well avoid the challenge (especially if they think others will succeed). This can be seen in classrooms every day. A large number of students decide that, taking all things into account, they would rather be thought lazy than dumb, and they refuse to engage with the task. This is a direct consequence of a fixed mindset.

In contrast, those who see ability as *incremental*—having what Dweck (2006) calls a *growth mindset*—see all challenges as chances to learn, to get smarter. These students will try harder in the face of failure. These two views of ability are generally not global—a student can believe that ability in mathematics is fixed but that ability in athletics is incremental, such that the more he or she practices, say, triple jump, the more his or her ability at that athletic endeavor will increase. Therefore, what we as teachers need to do is ensure that the feedback we give students supports a view of ability as incremental rather than fixed: by working, they're getting smarter.

> We as teachers need to . . . ensure that the feedback we give students supports a view of ability as incremental rather than fixed—making sure they understand that by working, they're getting smarter. (Wiliam, 2018, p. 136)

Your words go a long way toward supporting or discouraging fixed or growth mindsets. Students look to you as the authority on intelligence. After all, you are "judging" their intelligence with every grade you give them. To help students move away from this belief and promote a growth mindset, you may need to reframe some of your phrasing. Emphasize the importance of effort, and explain that mistakes are a natural part of learning. Don't praise students for natural ability. Rather, commend them for putting forth the effort to continuously learn. Take a look at the phrases in figure 4.4 and reframe them to encourage a growth mindset. Then, for the next couple of days, pay attention to how you phrase feedback to your students. Are there any phrases that you could reframe? Write them down in the blank spaces at the end of this figure. Writing such things down helps us to become more conscious of their use.

Praise

Students can also consider praise as feedback. Thomas L. Good and Douglas A. Grouws's (1975) seminal research shows clearly that praise is not necessarily a good thing—in fact, the best teachers appear to praise slightly less than average. It is the quality rather than the quantity of praise that is important, and teacher praise is far more effective if it is infrequent, credible, contingent, specific, and genuine (Brophy, 1981). For instance, instead of saying, "Great job!" try to be more specific and point out effort, as in, "I like the way you kept working at that math problem and trying different strategies until you got it!" It is also essential that teachers relate praise to factors within an individual's control, so praising a gifted student simply for being gifted—something the student cannot control—is likely to lead to negative consequences in the long term (Dweck, 2006). Table 4.2 provides examples of effective and ineffective praise. Individually or in your team, voice the differences in each pair.

Original Phrase	Reframed for Growth Mindset
You're a great mathematician.	
Just do your best.	
You're so smart!	
Some people just aren't good at writing.	
This quiz is really easy.	

Figure 4.4: Reframing phrases to promote growth mindsets.

Visit **go.SolutionTree.com/assessment** *for a free reproducible version of this figure.*

Table 4.2: Effective Versus Ineffective Praise

Effective Praise	Ineffective Praise
The details you included in your theme made me feel like I was right there.	Awesome work!
It seems like you're the one everyone turns to with their computer problems. Thanks for sharing your skills with your classmates.	You're so good with computers!
That example you just gave was one I never would have thought of, and you're exactly right.	That works. Good job!
This paper clearly demonstrates you've attained mastery in this concept. That is something to be proud of!	A+

Source: Silver, 2012.

Using praise can increase motivation, but then it becomes necessary to use praise all the time to maintain the motivation. In this situation, it is very difficult to maintain praise as genuine and sincere. In contrast, using feedback improves performance when it focuses on what needs to be done to improve, and particularly when it gives specific details about *how* to improve.

Feedback in the Form of Scaffolding

Sometimes less is more. Feedback that provides students with information about the correct answer to something that students answer incorrectly is the equivalent of restudying the material. This can help learning, because every time students recall an answer, their storage strength increases, but feedback is likely to be *more* effective if it helps students retrieve things themselves. Essentially, hints are likely to be more effective than answers.

As well as saving the teacher time, developing skills of intervening as little as possible—just enough to get the students going—promotes better learning. When students get stuck, try giving them a scaffolded response rather than the entire solution. Jonathon Saphier (2005), founder and president of Research for Better Teaching, provides a good example of this kind of feedback:

> Teacher: "What part don't you understand?"
>
> Student: "I just don't get it."
>
> Teacher: "Well, the first part is just like the last problem you did. Then we add one more variable. See if you can find out what it is, and I'll come back in a few minutes." (p. 92)

> Does it make a difference whether a teacher gives feedback orally or in writing? . . . From their observations, the researchers indicate that whether the teacher gives feedback orally or in writing is much less important than the fact that [students are] given time, in class, to use the feedback to improve their work. (Wiliam, 2018, pp. 128–129)

Teachers often think immediate feedback is better (Bjork, 1994), and this seems to be because they fail to distinguish between the level of *performance* in the learning task and the amount of *learning* that takes place. When we give students lots of support (in the form of feedback) to complete a particular task, then the level of the students' performance on that task increases. However, the amount of learning that takes place (the increase in memory storage strength) decreases because the student is not having to work so hard. Conversely, when students have to struggle in the learning task, the quality of their performance on the task reduces, but the amount of learning that takes place increases. In general, there is an inverse relationship between the quality of performance on a task and the amount of learning that occurs from completing that task.

For example, when providing feedback, avoid giving the students only marks that show the number of correct or incorrect answers. Instead, tell them that there are three incorrect answers and they have to find and fix them; this can be done individually or in small groups. This particular technique works well in mathematics, as there is typically a right or wrong solution. In English language arts, for example, you can mark a paragraph or sentence that contains an error and have them find and fix it. Explore different ways to provide feedback that scaffolds the learning rather than simply providing the correct solutions.

Are you working harder than your students? Let's find out. Using figure 4.5, keep track of the type of support you are giving students. With your busy schedule, you may be tempted to skip this exercise as it can seem a bit inconvenient, but we encourage you to track your feedback for at least a full day. Every time a student asks for help, simply mark the appropriate box for the type of support you provided. Awareness of your own practices is invaluable in making changes to meet your students' needs.

So far, out of all the feedback options available to teachers, we recommend three: (1) phrasing feedback to encourage incremental (or growth) rather than fixed mindsets; (2) dispensing infrequent, genuine, and specific praise; and (3) providing students with scaffolding opportunities, rather than solutions. All the research indicates that providing effective feedback is very difficult. Get it wrong, and students will give up, reject the feedback, or choose an easier goal. Even when students engage with the feedback, there is still a danger that the focus will shift to short-term rather than long-term goals. To avoid this danger, teachers should aim for feedback that they can use *formatively*—something that the practices of high-achieving sports coaches illustrate exceptionally.

Scaffold	Solution
Total:	**Total:**

Figure 4.5: Scaffolding versus providing the solution.

*Visit **go.SolutionTree.com/assessment** for a free reproducible version of this figure.*

Formative Feedback

Athletics coaches tend to see their jobs not as just identifying talent but also nurturing it and even producing it, often getting out of athletes more than the athletes themselves believe they could achieve. Coaches do this by providing *feedback that moves learning forward*. Instead of simply telling an athlete to score more points, coaches show their athletes how to score more points—providing the step-by-step actions that will produce a better play.

In their publication "Inside the Black Box," Paul Black and Dylan Wiliam (1998b) recommend that feedback during learning be in the form of comments rather than grades, and many teachers take this to heart. Unfortunately, in many cases, the feedback is not particularly helpful. Typically, the feedback focuses on what is deficient about the work students submit, which the students are not able to resubmit, rather than on what to do to improve their future learning. In such situations, feedback is rather like the scene in the rearview mirror rather than the one through the windshield. Or, as Douglas Reeves (2008) so memorably observes, it's like the difference between having a medical exam and a postmortem.

Feedback functions formatively *only if the learner uses the information to improve performance*. If educators intend the information to be helpful but the learner cannot use it to improve his or her performance, it is not formative. For example, telling a student that he or she needs to be more systematic in planning his or her scientific inquiries is not formative if the learner doesn't know *how* to be more systematic. This kind of feedback is *accurate*—correctly describing what needs to happen—but it is not *helpful* because the learner does not know how to use the feedback to improve. It is like telling an unsuccessful comedian to be funnier—accurate, but not particularly helpful, advice.

> The secret of effective feedback is that saying what's wrong isn't enough; to be effective, feedback must provide a *recipe for future action.*
> (Wiliam, 2018, p. 141)

To be effective as a recipe for future action, educators must design feedback to progress learning. In other words, the feedback must embody a model of progression, and here, again, is where coaching in athletics programs is well designed. It is not enough to simply clarify the current state and the goal state. The coach has to design a series of activities that will move athletes from their current state to the goal state. Often coaches will take a complex activity, such as the double play in baseball, and break it down into a series of components, each of which athletes need to practice until they reach fluency. They will then assemble the components together. Not only does the coach have a clear notion of quality (the well-executed double play), he or she also understands the *anatomy* of quality: he or she is able to see the high-quality performance as being composed of a series of elements that can be broken down into a developmental sequence for the athlete.

This skill of being able to break down a long learning journey—from the individual's current state to where he or she needs to be—into a series of small steps takes years for even the most capable coaches to develop. The best coaches claim they are always learning how to be better at coaching. However, there are clear principles of effective formative feedback that can guide their development. If teachers are to enhance the quality of their feedback, they, too, should follow the principles as follows.

- Feedback should be more work for the recipient than the donor.
- Feedback should be focused.
- Feedback should relate to shared learning goals.

We will now discuss each of these principles individually.

Feedback Should Be More Work for the Recipient Than the Donor

The first fundamental principle of effective classroom feedback is that feedback should be more work for the recipient than the donor. If we embrace the idea of feedback as a recipe for future action, then it is easy to see how to make feedback work constructively: don't provide students with feedback unless you allow them time, in class, to work on using the feedback to improve their work. Then, feedback does not evaluate how well or how badly one's work was done, but rather asks, "What's next?"

One technique for asking, "What's next?"—which is particularly effective when responding to a piece of student writing—is *three questions*. As the teacher reads each student's work, when she sees an item on which she would like the student to reflect, she places a numbered circle at that point in the text. Underneath the student's work, the teacher writes three questions, each relating to the relevant numbered circles, and leaves

1. _____
   _____
   _____

   Response: _____
   _____
   _____

2. _____
   _____
   _____

   Response: _____
   _____
   _____

3. _____
   _____
   _____

   Response: _____
   _____
   _____

Figure 4.6: Three questions template.

*Visit **go.SolutionTree.com/assessment** for a free reproducible version of this figure.*

space for the student's response. Then, the student takes the first ten or fifteen minutes of the next lesson to respond to the three questions. The important feature of this technique is that no matter how bad or good the student's work was, everyone has the same amount of work to do. Feedback is no longer a postmortem, but now more like a medical exam. Reproduce figure 4.6 to try this technique with your next batch of student writing.

Feedback Should Be Focused

A second principle of effective feedback is that it should be focused. We generally give our students large amounts of what we call feedback (although an engineer probably wouldn't), but it is usually of moderate quality, and we generally don't require students to respond to it. In giving feedback, less is often more. A lot of feedback (or corrections, as students often view it) can overwhelm many students. However, if we focus on feedback that is most important to the learning goal or intention, rather than point out every small discrepancy in the work, then students are more likely to see the feedback as manageable and work toward higher achievement.

Feedback Should Relate to Shared Learning Goals

To be effective, feedback needs to direct attention to what's next rather than focusing on how well or poorly the student did on the work. . . . In many classrooms, teachers require students to do corrections for homework, leaving high achievers with nothing to do. Used in this way, feedback really is punishment. (Wiliam, 2018, p. 143)

Following this same line of thinking, the third principle is that feedback should relate to the learning goals that the teacher has shared with students. If a teacher provides a scoring rubric, then it is important that the feedback relates to that rubric. If there are learning intentions and success criteria for the work, then the feedback should relate back to those. This sounds obvious, but teachers often provide students with rubrics or success criteria and yet fail to use these in framing their feedback to the students.

If we had to reduce all the research on feedback into one simple overarching idea, at least for academic subjects in school, it would be this: *feedback should cause thinking*. All the practical techniques this chapter discusses work because, in one way or another, they get the students to think about, rather than react emotionally to, the feedback they receive.

In Your Classroom

This chapter describes some ways to give effective feedback, but you (and every teacher) will be able to come up with many more, provided that you heed the key lessons provided here. Let's start with just one though. Using figure 4.7, make a plan to incorporate this strategy in your classroom.

If we are to harness the power of feedback to increase student learning, then we need to ensure that feedback causes a cognitive, not an emotional, reaction—in other words, feedback should cause thinking. Feedback should be focused, it should relate to the learning goals that teachers share with students, and it should be more work for the recipient than the donor. Indeed, the whole purpose of feedback should be to increase the extent to which students are owners of their own learning, which we learn about in the next chapter.

Strategy: Providing Feedback That Moves Learning Forward
Lesson:
Technique:
Expectations and goals for using this technique:
Results:
Modifications for future use:

Figure 4.7: Plan for providing feedback that moves learning forward.

*Visit **go.SolutionTree.com/assessment** for a free reproducible version of this figure.*

Discussion Questions

You may answer the following questions independently or with your team to reinforce the chapter's key points.

1. In your own words, describe feedback that is useful to students.

2. In what ways do you currently provide feedback to your students? Is it effective? How do you know?

3. How important is it to promote a growth, or incremental, mindset in your students?

4. What technique from this chapter would you like to try, and why does it make sense for your students?

Chapter 5

Activating Learners as Instructional Resources for One Another

Even though there is a substantial body of research (such as Barkley, Cross, & Major, 2005; Cohen & Lotan, 2014; Slavin, Hurley, & Chamberlain, 2003) that demonstrates the extraordinary power of collaborative and cooperative learning to produce tangible and substantial increases in students' learning, educators rarely deploy these practices effectively in classrooms. This chapter discusses how teachers can effectively enable students to work together to become meaningful, valuable resources for each other's learning. Note that it is not our intent to enter the argument of whether students can give each other accurate grades or not. The focus in this chapter is on helping students at all levels *improve*, rather than evaluate, the work of their peers—and as a result, heighten their own learning. This chapter will explore the role that learners can play in improving their peers' learning and conclude with a number of specific classroom techniques that educators can use to put these principles into practice.

Current Practice

Let's take a moment to review our current practices for activating students as instructional resources for one another. Use figure 5.1 (page 72) to note all relevant practices and how well you believe they work in your classroom.

Cooperative Learning

Having reviewed the evidence, Robert E. Slavin, Eric A. Hurley, and Anne Chamberlain (2003) conclude that "research on cooperative learning is one of the greatest success stories in the history of educational research" (p. 177). Exactly why cooperative learning has such a profound effect is still a matter of some debate, although there appear to be four key factors (Wiliam, 2018).

Practice	Effectiveness	Notes

Figure 5.1: Inventory of current practices for the strategy of activating learners as instructional resources for one another.

*Visit **go.SolutionTree.com/assessment** for a free reproducible version of this figure.*

1. **Motivation:** Students help their peers learn because, in well-structured cooperative learning settings, it is in their own interests to do so, and so effort increases.

2. **Social cohesion:** Students help their peers because they care about the group, again leading to increased effort.

3. **Personalization:** Students learn more because their more able peers can engage with the particular difficulties a student is having.

4. **Cognitive elaboration:** Students who provide help in group settings have to think through the ideas more clearly. (p. 156)

Effective cooperative learning requires the presence of two elements (Slavin et al., 2003). First, there must be group goals, so that students are working *as* a group, not merely *in* a group. Second, there must be individual accountability, so that individual students cannot be carried along by the work of others.

Studies find that both low achievers and high achievers benefit from cooperative learning environments (for example, Barkley et al., 2005; Cohen & Lotan, 2014). Overall, it appears that cooperative learning is equally effective for students at all achievement levels as long as two key elements—(1) group goals and (2) individual accountability—are present (Slavin et al., 2003).

Although these two elements—group goals and individual accountability—seem straightforward, they cut across some widely held assumptions about fairness for groups and individuals. For example, most teachers accept the idea of group rewards for behavior as fair. Using peer pressure to promote good behavior seems to be broadly acceptable.

> The effect of peer tutoring can be almost as strong as one-on-one instruction from a teacher. John Schacter's (2000) study . . . finds that students working in student-led groups learn almost as much as students getting one-on-one tutorial instruction from a teacher, and those in student-led groups actually learn more than those in teacher-led groups. (Wiliam, 2018, p. 157)

However, the practice is markedly less acceptable when applied to academic work. For example, imagine a situation where, at the end of the week, a teacher quizzes his or her class, and each group receives the lowest-scoring group member's score (of course, the teacher doesn't reveal the lowest-scoring member's name). In other words, the achievement at the *trailing edge* applies to the whole group.

Many teachers (not to mention students and parents) find this type of assessment completely unacceptable. They point out that the score they award to the group, being that of the lowest-scoring member, does not represent the group's level of achievement—an entirely fair point. It would certainly be invalid to infer anything about the individual group members' achievement from this score, and it would be quite wrong to enter this score in a gradebook as a record of the individual group members' achievement. But if, instead, the teacher and student take the score to indicate how well the students worked *as a group*, then the awarded score seems more reasonable.

The fact that many teachers view group rewards for good behavior as entirely legitimate but trailing-edge scoring as unacceptable reveals how difficult it is to achieve the benefits of cooperative learning in classrooms. In fact, research shows that what teachers describe as cooperative learning in their classrooms rarely has the features that would make it effective. One survey shows that of twenty-one teachers who state they were implementing

One objection to cooperative learning is that it holds back the able students. However, if the students engaged in peer tutoring are providing elaborated explanations rather than just answers, then there is compelling evidence that both those who give and those who receive help will benefit. (Wiliam, 2018, p. 164)

cooperative learning, only five implement the learning in such a way as to create both group goals and individual accountability (Antil, Jenkins, Wayne, & Vadasy, 1998). And only one of the twenty-one teachers implement cooperative learning that satisfies the more complex criteria Elizabeth G. Cohen (1994) proposes: namely, open-ended tasks that emphasize higher-order thinking, group tasks that require input from other members, multiple tasks related to a central intellectual theme, and roles assigned to different group members. This lack of *true* cooperative learning in classrooms means that students are failing to take ownership of their own learning and to find that intrinsic motivation to achieve their goals.

Collaboration Techniques

Because cooperative learning is a rather tricky strategy, both to design appropriately and to implement, we'll explore a number of techniques that teachers find useful in getting started with the process of activating students as learning resources for one another. Remember, the purpose of peer assessment should be, simply and purely, to help the individual being assessed improve his or her work.

Elaborated Explanations

Elaborated explanations involve explaining why a particular answer is correct, rather than just giving the correct answer to a peer. Researchers find that both those giving and getting help benefit from this technique, and the benefit is especially great for those giving help, producing at least a 50 percent increase in the rate of learning (Webb, 1991).

Half-Ability Groups

It is a common assumption that students who learn most in group work are those who give help and those who receive it (provided, of course, that the help is in the form of elaborated explanations, rather than just answers; see Webb, 1991). If there is a large range of ability within a group, students in the middle risk becoming disengaged spectators, watching the high achievers teach the low achievers. They don't need the help that the weakest students need, but they also aren't forced to articulate their thinking as the strongest students are when they teach others. Thus, teachers may choose to organize students into half-ability groups—weak achievers with middle, and middle with strong—to engage as many students as possible in an activity that helps learning.

C3B4ME

In this technique, a student must ask at least three other students for help before seeking it from the teacher, hence the description *see three before me* (C3B4ME). Of course, you need to encourage a collaborative learning environment for this. Often, students don't feel comfortable talking to other students in class, as a quiet and orderly classroom has traditionally been the ideal environment, and teachers often discipline talkative students for talking to their classmates. Students may also be skeptical about this, thinking it could be considered cheating. To show that you are serious about changing the classroom contract, have students sign the form in figure 5.2, which grants permission for assistance from classmates.

In this classroom, there is more than one teacher in the room! Students will seek help from three other students before asking me for help. This applies to practice work only. Exams are excluded.

Teacher: _____

Student: _____

Figure 5.2: C3B4ME technique contract.

*Visit **go.SolutionTree.com/assessment** for a free reproducible version of this figure.*

You can regularly require students to discuss problems in pairs or small groups before participating in all-class discussions to stimulate this culture shift.

Peer Improvement of Homework

Peer improvement of homework can take many forms. Sometimes the teacher gives the students a rubric, and they have to assess their own homework against that rubric. Sometimes the teacher tells students to swap notebooks with a neighbor and assess each other's, and sometimes the teacher asks one group of students to look at another group's work. Some teachers mix it up, and students don't know which practice will take place from day to day.

This technique has several benefits. First, it lessens the teacher's load. He or she doesn't have to spend time checking each student's homework. Second, students are more likely to actually do the homework. Students don't like to be left out of class activities, and if they do not do the work, they do not get to participate. Third, students are more likely to put forth effort. The peer pressure to do a good job is a strong motivator for not only doing the work, but also doing good work.

> To improve the quality of [peer] feedback, a teacher collects examples of feedback from the class, displays each example to the class (anonymously), then asks the class to vote on whether it thinks that the comment would be useful to them. The class then discusses the salient features of the best-rated feedback, and the teacher displays the resulting criteria on a poster in the classroom for future reference. (Wiliam, 2018)

Note that because students will be tempted to give their friends higher grades than perhaps what is called for, this technique should only be used on practice work that is not going to be given a grade for the gradebook. Emphasize to students that this practice is intended to help each other learn. You may want to periodically check on their assessments to ensure they are providing the correct feedback.

Homework Help Board

This technique is pretty self-explanatory. Students indicate on the homework help board any questions that they have about the homework. Teachers encourage students who think they can help students who have questions about the homework to seek those students out and provide help. Use figure 5.3 as a trial sign-up sheet. If this technique works for your class, you may want to let the students collaborate to create their own system for the homework help board.

If your students are uncomfortable announcing to the class that they need help, you may want to assign a number to each question instead of the student's name. Once a student helper signs up to help with the question, provide him or her with the name of the student who needs assistance. Gradually, students will become more comfortable with asking for help if they see that others are using this resource as well.

Two Stars and a Wish

> When allowing students to comment on their classmates' work, you may want to consider giving them sticky notes to use. Students can write the comments on sticky notes so that if the recipient doesn't find the feedback helpful, he or she can easily remove it. (Wiliam, 2018)

This technique requires that when any student gives feedback on another student's work, he or she has to provide two things he or she thinks are good about the work (the two stars) and a suggestion for improvement (the wish). Reproduce figure 5.4 (page 78) for students to fill out.

End-of-Topic Questions

It is quite common for a teacher to reach the end of a chapter or a unit and ask the class, "Any questions?" Of course, few students are willing to ask a question because they do not want to look foolish in front of the class. To overcome this, the teacher can instead say, "In your groups, decide if you have any questions." Just the chance to talk through the matter with their peers can give students more confidence when asking questions in front of the class. Some teachers go even further and insist that each group must come up with at least one question. The teacher then collects the questions, sorts them quickly, and deals with all the questions on the same issue at the same time.

Error Classification

This technique is useful when you can classify errors in a straightforward way. For example, a Spanish teacher may collect drafts of a piece of writing in Spanish, use a pencil to underline errors in the text, and return the work to the students. The students then have to classify the errors they have made (for example, tense, gender, pronouns, and possessives). After classifying their errors and determining the areas in which they made few errors, students identify a buddy with complementary strengths to help them correct their work.

Student Reporter

Five minutes before the lesson ends, split the class into groups and ask each group to produce a list of things it learned during the lesson. Each group then reports to the class one thing it has learned.

An alternative is to have a student reporter lead the end-of-lesson discussion. The student reporter summarizes the lesson's main points and tries to answer any remaining questions that students in the class may have (one teacher calls the student reporter *the captain* so the lesson summary is the *captain's log*). If he or she can't answer the questions, then the reporter asks members of the class to help out.

Question	Student	Student Helper

Figure 5.3: Homework help sign-up sheet.

*Visit **go.SolutionTree.com/assessment** for a free reproducible version of this figure.*

Figure 5.4: Two stars and a wish template.

*Visit **go.SolutionTree.com/assessment** for a free reproducible version of this figure.*

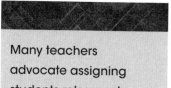

Many teachers advocate assigning students roles, such as chair, timekeeper, facilitator, scribe, and so on, when they are working collaboratively. This can be a good idea, but in general, it is a bad idea to assign the role of reporter at the outset. As soon as students know that someone else will have to report back, they can ease off, as the need for individual accountability weakens. (Wiliam, 2018, pp. 163–164)

Preflight Checklist

Before a student can submit an assignment, a buddy must sign off on it after checking that all the features the teacher requires are present. When the teacher grades the assignment, if any items on the preflight checklist are not up to standard, it is the buddy, rather than the student submitting the assignment, who is taken to task, thus creating a measure of accountability for the buddy to take the task seriously. Fill in the first column of figure 5.5 and pass a copy out to students for each assignment. Have the student buddy place a check mark in the Met or Not Yet column for each criterion.

I-You-We Checklist

At the end of a group activity, each student makes note of something about his or her own contributions, something about other individuals' contributions, and an evaluation of the whole group's quality of work (hence, *I-you-we*). Use figure 5.6 (page 80) as a template for this technique.

Group-Based Test Preparation

When students are preparing for a test, teachers can make reviewing more engaging by organizing students into groups of five or six and assigning each student one aspect of the work to review. The following day, each member presents to the group and answers questions about his or her particular topic. As the other students are relying on the information to prepare them for an upcoming exam, peer pressure is a great motivation to learn the content inside and out.

Requirement	Met	Not Yet

Figure 5.5: Preflight checklist template.

*Visit **go.SolutionTree.com/assessment** for a free reproducible version of this figure.*

Lesson:
Date:
My contributions to the activity:
My group mates' contributions to the activity:
Things we did well:
Things we need to work on:

Figure 5.6: I-You-We checklist template.

*Visit **go.SolutionTree.com/assessment** for a free reproducible version of this figure.*

In Your Classroom

This chapter has presented a number of classroom techniques that teachers can use with students of almost any grade and that they can readily incorporate into practice. It's time to choose one that you believe will resonate with your students. Use figure 5.7 (page 82) to make your plan.

Many techniques for this strategy focus specifically on peer assessment, which can be especially powerful if teachers gear it toward improvement rather than evaluation—students tend to be much more direct with each other than any teacher would dare to be. However, it is important to realize that peer assessment also benefits the individual who provides the help. Making students give feedback to each other forces them to internalize the learning intentions and success criteria, but in the context of someone else's work, which is much less emotionally charged. Activating students as learning resources for one another can, therefore, be seen as a stepping stone to students becoming owners of their own learning, which we discuss in the next chapter.

Strategy: Activating Learners as Instructional Resources for One Another
Lesson:
Technique:
Expectations and goals for using this technique:
Results:
Modifications for future use:

Figure 5.7: Plan for activating learners as instructional resources for one another.

*Visit **go.SolutionTree.com/assessment** for a free reproducible version of this figure.*

Discussion Questions

You may answer the following questions independently or with your team to reinforce the chapter's key points.

1. How comfortable are you with allowing students to assess each other's work?

2. What are the advantages and disadvantages of cooperative learning?

3. In what ways can you ensure that students are using their collaborative time to help each other learn?

4. What technique from this chapter would you like to try, and why does it make sense for your students?

Chapter 6

Activating Learners as Owners of Their Own Learning

Teachers do not create learning; only learners create learning (Wiliam, 2018). And yet our classrooms seem to be based on the opposite principle—that if they try really hard, teachers can do the learning for the learners. Accountability regimes that mandate sanctions for teachers, for schools, and for districts, but not for students, exacerbate this. Getting students more involved in their learning and activating students as owners of their own learning can improve their achievement extraordinarily. This chapter will show you how to encourage self-regulated learning in your classroom and will also provide multiple techniques for student self-reflection.

Current Practice

Let's take a moment to review our current practices for activating students as owners of their own learning. What does the phrase "Activating students as owners of their own learning" mean to you and your students? If you haven't thought in these terms before, you might find it helpful to discuss the concept with a colleague. Use figure 6.1 (page 86) to note all your current learning activation practices and how well you believe they work in your classroom.

Can students develop sufficient insights into their own learning to improve it? The answer is yes, and this is what this strategy intends. The big idea here is that students should be taking more responsibility for their own learning, so that over time, they are able to manage their own learning as well as, or even better, than any teacher could. In other words, in psychological jargon, they become self-regulating learners.

Self-Regulated Learning

Self-regulated learning enables the learner to coordinate cognitive resources, emotions, and actions in the pursuit of his or her learning goals (Boekaerts, 2006). Some emphasize the cognitive aspects of this process

Practice	Effectiveness	Notes

Figure 6.1: Inventory of current practices for the strategy of activating learners as owners of their own learning.

*Visit **go.SolutionTree.com/assessment** for a free reproducible version of this figure.*

(for example, Winne, 1996)—does the learner have the necessary knowledge, skills, strategies, and so on to reach the goal? Others point out that many students possess the necessary skills but do not use them in classrooms, which suggests that the problem is not a lack of skill but rather a lack of motivation or volition (for example, Corno, 2001). This section will discuss two student attributes necessary for self-regulation—(1) metacognition and (2) motivation—and how they interact. It will also discuss how teachers can use these attributes to inspire a growth, rather than fixed, mindset in their students for optimal student learning.

> Self-regulated learning enables the learner to coordinate cognitive resources, emotions, and actions in the service of his or her learning goals (Boekaerts, 2006).

Metacognition

John H. Flavell (1976), widely credited with inventing the term *metacognition*, defines it as follows: "'Metacognition' refers to one's knowledge concerning one's own cognitive processes and products or anything related to them, e.g., the learning-relevant properties of information and data" (p. 232). Metacognition includes knowing what one knows (*metacognitive knowledge*), what one can do (*metacognitive skills*), and what one knows about one's own cognitive abilities (*metacognitive experience*). The research shows clearly that "how well students do in school can be determined by how well they are able to self-regulate" (Shanker, 2013, p. ix) and, more important, that training students in metacognition raises their performance (for example, Bol, Campbell, Perez, & Yen, 2016) and allows them to generalize what they have learned to novel contexts (Hacker, Dunlosky, & Graesser, 1998). In short, self-regulated learning creates successful students because they are invested in their learning—"self-regulation of learning involves more than detailed knowledge of a skill; it involves the self-awareness, self-motivation, and behavioral skill to implement that knowledge appropriately" (Zimmerman, 2002, p. 66).

While it may seem that teachers can do little to "teach" metacognition, there are several ways that they can encourage the strengthening of the metacognitive skills that students inherently possess. For instance, developmental psychologist Marilyn Price-Mitchell (2015) suggests educators teach students about their brains and how they are wired for growth; allow students to be confused and recognize what they don't understand; provide opportunities for reflection; have students keep journals about how they learn rather than what they learn; and offer essay exams rather than multiple-choice exams, requiring students to use metacognitive skills to prepare for the exams. However, these skills will be useful only if students are motivated to use them.

Motivation

Much of the literature about motivation in schools treats motivation like a substance in students' brains: some students have a lot of it, and others don't. When students fail to learn, we thus blame their lack of motivation. At the other extreme, some believe that it is the teacher's job to motivate the students. Thus, if the students don't learn, it is because the teacher was not a sufficiently good motivator, so the cause of the failure to learn is the teacher.

However, there is another way to think about motivation—not as a cause but as a *consequence* of achievement. This way of thinking is particularly marked in psychologist Mihaly Csikszentmihalyi's work. In his book *Flow: The Psychology of Optimal Experience*, Csikszentmihalyi (1990) describes various situations in which individuals became completely absorbed in the activities in which they engage. He describes this state of complete absorption in an activity as *flow*. This sense of flow can arise because of one's intrinsic interest in a task, but it can also arise through a match between one's capability and the task's challenge level. Boredom occurs when one's level of challenge is low and one's level of capability is high. Anxiety results when the level of challenge is high and the level of capability is low. Apathy results when both are low. However, flow results when levels of both capability and challenge are high (Spencer, 2016).

This way of thinking about motivation is radical because it does not locate the problem in either the teacher or the learner, but rather in the match between challenge and capability. Traditionally, the student or teacher is at fault when the student lacks motivation. But if we see motivation not as a cause but as an *outcome*, an emergent property of getting the match between challenge and capability right, then if the student lacks motivation, that's just a signal that the teacher and the learner need to try something different.

This is to say that although students' motivation and their belief in their ability to carry their plans through to successful completion—what psychologist Albert Bandura (1997) terms *self-efficacy*—tends to decline as students go through school, what the teacher does can make a real difference. The teacher's actions, then, depend on an understanding of how the motivational and cognitive perspectives around learning act, and also how they interact.

Motivational and Cognitive Perspectives Integrated

This discussion may appear to have brought us a long distance from classroom formative assessment, but in order to fulfill the potential of formative assessment, we must recognize that assessment is a two-edged sword. Assessment can improve instruction, but it can also affect the learner's willingness, desire, and capacity to learn (Harlen & Crick, 2002). Although we don't yet know everything about the most effective learning environments, the existing research on cognition and motivation provides clear and strong evidence that activating students as owners of their own learning is an essential component.

When educators invite students to participate in a learning activity, students use several sources of information to decide what they are going to do (Wiliam, 2018).

- **Current perceptions of the task:** Does this look like a task I can successfully complete?

- **Previous experiences on similar tasks:** Have I undertaken similar tasks before and was I successful or not? Did I enjoy them?

- **Beliefs about the subject or task:** Is this a subject or a task that I think I am good at, or is it a subject that I know I find difficult?

- **Beliefs about "ability" and the role of effort in the subject:** Is this a subject that I think I need to be really smart to be successful in or is it a subject where I can be successful if I try really hard?

- **Interest in the subject (personal versus situational):** Is this a subject or a topic that I am interested in (personal interest)? Has the task been presented in a way that makes me interested in undertaking it (situational interest)?

- **Costs and benefits:** How much effort will I have to put into this task to be successful? Will it be worth it? How will I feel if I try my best and do not succeed? Will I be embarrassed or would it be OK to try and still fail? Is it likely that others will succeed? (pp. 178–179)

The students then weigh the information and begin to channel energy along one of two pathways, focusing either on growth or well-being (Boekaerts, 1993). This decision, however, is dynamic and can change rapidly. For example, after giving some attention to well-being, a student may find a way to lower the threat to self-image, thus allowing a shift of energy and attention back to the growth pathway.

The motivational and cognitive perspectives on self-regulated learning can be brought together within Monique Boekaerts's (1993) dual-processing self-regulation model. The dual-processing self-regulation model suggests that the most important thing is creating learning environments that encourage students to activate the growth rather than the well-being pathway. We cannot possibly anticipate all the factors that a student may take into account in deciding whether to pursue growth rather than well-being, but there are a number of things that teachers can do to tip the scales in the right direction (Wiliam, 2018).

- Share learning goals with students so that they are able to monitor their own progress toward them. (See also chapter 1, page 3.)

- Promote the belief that ability is incremental rather than fixed. When students think they can't get smarter, they are likely to devote their energy to avoiding failure. (See also Growth Mindset and Fixed Mindset, page 61.)

- Make it more difficult for students to compare their achievement with others.

- Provide feedback that contains a recipe for future action rather than a review of past failures (a medical exam rather than a postmortem). (See also Formative Feedback, page 65.)

- Use every opportunity to transfer executive control of the learning from the teacher to the students to support their development as autonomous learners.

Where do you stand on each item? Use figure 6.2 to reflect on your current practices and find areas that you may need to strengthen.

Practice	Never	Sometimes	Always
Share learning goals with students so that they are able to monitor their own progress toward them.			
Promote the belief that ability is incremental rather than fixed. When students think they can't get smarter, they are likely to devote their energy to avoiding failure.			
Make it more difficult for students to compare their achievement with others.			
Provide feedback that contains a recipe for future action rather than a review of past failures (a medical exam rather than a postmortem).			
Use every opportunity to transfer executive control of the learning from the teacher to the students to support their development as autonomous learners.			

Figure 6.2: Self-assessment for promoting growth in the classroom.

*Visit **go.SolutionTree.com/assessment** for a free reproducible version of this figure.*

The fact that we know what needs to be done is not the same as actually doing it. Continuously developing one's teaching is extremely difficult. The good news is that you need not start from scratch. Rather, building on the achievements of other teachers who have already developed techniques, such as those in the next section, will help you encourage the growth pathway or mindset in your students.

Techniques for Student Self-Reflection

Following are some techniques that encourage students to reflect on their own learning. We will discuss four techniques.

1. Self-testing

2. Traffic lights

3. Learning portfolios

4. Learning logs

Self-Testing

There is now increasing evidence that having students assess themselves is one of the most straightforward and inexpensive ways to increase student achievement, especially when this is done through self-testing. (See, for example, Dunlosky, Rawson, Marsh, Nathan, & Willingham, 2013; Metcalfe, Butterfield, Habeck, & Stern, 2012.) Practice testing gives students practice in retrieving things from memory and therefore increases long-term memory (*storage strength*).

> There is no doubt that activating students as owners of their own learning produces substantial increases in learning, but it is not a quick fix. Many teachers find that students' first attempts at self-assessment are usually neither insightful nor useful. (Wiliam, 2018, p. 180)

A second benefit of practice testing, which comes when students find out if they were correct or not, is known as the *hypercorrection effect*—"general information errors that people commit with a high degree of belief [confidence] are especially easy to correct" (Metcalfe et al., 2012, p. 1571). So, if students complete a practice test and immediately get feedback on their answers, students will benefit from the hypercorrection effect for those questions where they were confident they were correct, and they will thus be more likely to score correctly on the second test.

The problem with self-testing, of course, is that students do not like tests, and students will likely greet with dismay any attempt to increase the amount of testing. The solution to this dilemma is realizing that students do not gain any additional benefit from practice testing when a score is recorded in a gradebook. We need more testing but less grading. Teachers should encourage students to test themselves, use practice tests, and check their own answers, but should not require students to tell anyone how well they did (unless they want to, of course).

Traffic Lights

Many teachers use a technique known as *traffic lights* to activate students as owners of their own learning. At the beginning of the lesson, the teacher shares the learning intentions and any associated success criteria with the students, and at the end of the period, the students assess the extent to which they have achieved the intended learning by placing a colored circle against the learning intention they wrote in their notebooks at the start of the lesson. Green indicates confidence that the student has achieved the learning intention. Yellow indicates either ambivalence about the extent to which the student has achieved the learning intention or that the student has partially met the objectives. Red indicates that the student believes that he or she has not learned the material.

Educators can use this technique in several different ways in the classroom, such as for test preparation. A teacher may encourage students to place a colored dot in the top corner of each page in their notebook to signal their confidence with the material on that page. When preparing for the test, students can then skip over or minimize study time spent on the material they flag as green and concentrate on those areas in which they are less confident.

Another modification of this technique may be to use red and green disks to acquire learning information in real time. A high school algebra teacher who has been using traffic lights for a while gives each student in the class a compact disc–sized disk, green on one side and red on the other. At the beginning of the period, the green side faces up, but, as the lesson progresses, if students want to signal that they think the teacher is going too fast, they flip the disk over to red. She finds that students who haven't asked a single question that year in class are willing to flip the disk over to red to show that they are getting confused. This allows her to modify her teaching immediately.

Another teacher tries the red and green disks but finds that the disks are difficult to see clearly from the front of his classroom due to fluorescent lighting. So he goes to a party store and buys colored cups in red, yellow, and green. In his classroom, he gives each student one of each colored cup, and the lesson begins with the green cup showing. If the student wants to signal that the teacher is going too fast, then the student shows the yellow cup. If a student wants to ask a question, then he or she displays the red cup. Why would any student show red? Because in this classroom, the rule is that as soon as one student shows red, the teacher uses the Popsicle sticks to pick another student at random, and the selected student has to go to the front of the classroom to answer the question the student who showed red poses.

This technique neatly encapsulates two integral components of effective formative assessment—engagement and responsiveness. If a student is showing yellow or green, the teacher can call on that student to explain the work to someone else, which requires the students to be monitoring their own learning and, therefore, be engaged. Additionally, the flow of information from the students about the pace of instruction helps the teacher make adjustments to be more responsive to the students' learning needs.

Learning Portfolios

A learning portfolio is useful for an incremental view of ability. When students do better work, the teacher adds work to the portfolio rather than replacing earlier work, to allow students to review their learning journeys. Looking back at earlier examples of their persuasive writing, for instance, can help students see what skills they have developed, which has two immediate benefits. First, seeing what has improved and thus identifying a trajectory of development means the student is likely to see how further improvement might be possible. Second, focusing on improvement means the student is more likely to see ability as incremental rather than fixed, which, as we learned previously, is a key characteristic of the most effective learners.

Have students fill out figure 6.3 to help them kick-start their self-reflection. It has a scale of one (beginning) to four (exemplary).

Learning Logs

One technique that many teachers find useful as a way of getting students to reflect on their learning is to ask them to complete a learning log at the end of a lesson. Of course, there is nothing new about learning logs, but some teachers find a slight variant on the usual method useful. Instead of providing responses to one or two self-assessment questions that you offer, invite students to respond to no more than three of the prompts in figure 6.4 (page 94). Getting students to choose which three of these statements they respond to seems to encourage a more thoughtful approach to the process of reflecting on learning.

Teachers have a crucial role to play when designing the situations in which learning takes place, but only learners create learning. Therefore, it is not surprising that the better the learners are able to manage their learning, the better they learn. All students can improve how they manage their learning processes and become owners of their own learning. However, this is not an easy process. Reflecting critically on one's own learning is emotionally charged, which is why developing such skills takes considerable time, especially with students who are accustomed to failure.

In Your Classroom

This final strategy—activating students as owners of their own learning—brings together all the other formative assessment strategies to create ideal learning conditions. Leading students to take responsibility for their own learning is helping them succeed both in and out of the classroom. Which technique from this chapter will you try in your classroom? Fill out figure 6.5 (page 95) to make a plan.

We know that the teacher is the most powerful influence on how much a student learns, and that teachers can continue to make significant improvements in their practice throughout their entire careers. If all teachers accept the need to improve practice, not because they are not good enough but because they can be even better, and focus on the things that will make the biggest difference to their students, we *will* be able to prepare our students to thrive in the impossibly complex, unpredictable world of the 21st century.

Scale: 1 = Beginning 2 = Developing 3 = Proficient 4 = Exemplary		
Learning intention:		
Success criterion:	**Beginning level:**	**Current level:**
	Evidence of progress:	
Success criterion:	**Beginning level:**	**Current level:**
	Evidence of progress:	
Success criterion:	**Beginning level:**	**Current level:**
	Evidence of progress:	
Success criterion:	**Beginning level:**	**Current level:**
	Evidence of progress:	
Success criterion:	**Beginning level:**	**Current level:**
	Evidence of progress:	

Figure 6.3: Self-assessment of progress using learning portfolios.

Today I learned . . .
I was surprised by . . .
The most useful thing I will take from this lesson is . . .
I was interested in . . .
What I liked most about this lesson was . . .
One thing I'm not sure about is . . .
The main thing I want to find out more about is . . .
After this session, I feel . . .
I might have gotten more from this lesson if . . .

Figure 6.4: Template for learning logs.

*Visit **go.SolutionTree.com/assessment** for a free reproducible version of this figure.*

Strategy: Activating Learners as Owners of Their Own Learning
Lesson:
Technique:
Expectations and goals for using this technique:
Results:
Modifications for future use:

Figure 6.5: Plan for activating learners as owners of their own learning.

Discussion Questions

You may answer the following questions independently or with your team to reinforce the chapter's key points.

1. What does it mean for students to own their own learning?

2. How do metacognition and motivation influence how you implement this strategy?

3. In what ways can this strategy aid students outside the classroom?

4. What technique from this chapter would you like to try, and why does it make sense for your students?

Appendix:
Observation Tools

As stated previously, while this book is a companion to *Embedded Formative Assessment, Second Edition* (Wiliam, 2018), we designed this book to also stand alone. This means that any individual teacher can pick it up and immediately use its tools and suggestions to implement the most effective formative assessment practices in his or her classroom. That being said, we believe that cooperative learning benefits teachers just as much as it does students, and, therefore, we suggest you work through this book with a colleague or teacher team. To aid in that process, we provide some collaboration tools here as well.

It can really help to have a colleague sit in on one of your classes to observe how you use formative assessment. As you have a lot going on in terms of delivering the lesson, checking for understanding, and providing intervention and enrichment when needed, you may find it difficult to remember everything that happened when it comes time to reflect on the practice. An observer can help. Observation is not meant as evaluation. Rather, we are asking the observer to simply watch for a particular practice taking place in the classroom and write down everything he or she witnesses during and as a result of that practice. Use the following reproducible observation tools for the formative assessment strategies. (Visit **go.SolutionTree.com/assessment** to download the free reproducibles in this book.)

Technique Observation Template: Clarifying, Sharing, and Understanding Learning Intentions and Success Criteria

Teacher:	Class or subject:	Date:

Strategy to observe: Clarifying, sharing, and understanding learning intentions and success criteria

Technique to observe:

Observer should focus on:

Observer's comments:

The Handbook for Embedded Formative Assessment © 2018 Solution Tree Press • SolutionTree.com

Visit **go.SolutionTree.com/assessment** to download this free reproducible.

Technique Observation Template:
Eliciting Evidence of Learners' Achievement

Teacher:	Class or subject:	Date:

Strategy to observe: Eliciting evidence of learners' achievement

Technique to observe:

Observer should focus on:

Observer's comments:

Technique Observation Template:
Providing Feedback That Moves Learning Forward

Teacher:	Class or subject:	Date:

Strategy to observe: Providing feedback that moves learning forward

Technique to observe:

Observer should focus on:

Observer's comments:

The Handbook for Embedded Formative Assessment © 2018 Solution Tree Press • SolutionTree.com

Visit **go.SolutionTree.com/assessment** to download this free reproducible.

Technique Observation Template:
Activating Learners as Instructional Resources for One Another

Teacher:	Class or subject:	Date:

Strategy to observe: Activating learners as instructional resources for one another

Technique to observe:

Observer should focus on:

Observer's comments:

Technique Observation Template:
Activating Learners as Owners of Their Own Learning

Teacher:	Class or subject:	Date:

Strategy to observe: Activating learners as owners of their own learning

Technique to observe:

Observer should focus on:

Observer's comments:

References and Resources

Antil, L. R., Jenkins, J. R., Wayne, S. K., & Vadasy, P. F. (1998). Cooperative learning: Prevalence, conceptualization and the relation between research and practice. *American Educational Research Journal, 35*(3), 419–454.

Arter, J. A., & McTighe, J. (2001). *Scoring rubrics in the classroom: Using performance criteria for assessing and improving student performance.* Thousand Oaks, CA: Corwin Press.

Ausubel, D. P. (1968). *Educational psychology: A cognitive view.* New York: Holt, Rinehart and Winston.

Bandura, A. (1997). *Self-efficacy: The exercise of control.* New York: Freeman.

Bangert-Drowns, R. L., Kulik, C.-L. C., Kulik, J. A., & Morgan, M. (1991). The instructional effect of feedback in test-like events. *Review of Educational Research, 61*(2), 213–238.

Barber, M., & Mourshed, M. (2007). *How the world's best-performing school systems come out on top.* London: McKinsey.

Barkley, E. F., Cross, K. P., & Major, C. H. (2005). *Collaborative learning techniques: A handbook for college faculty.* San Francisco: Jossey-Bass.

Barry, D. (Series Producer), & Hardy, E. (Executive Producer). (2010). *The classroom experiment* [Television series]. London: British Broadcasting.

Bennett, R. E. (2009). *A critical look at the meaning and basis of formative assessment* (ETS Research Memorandum No. RM-09–06). Princeton, NJ: Educational Testing Service.

Bjork, R. A. (1994). Memory and metamemory considerations in the training of human beings. In J. Metcalfe & A. P. Shimamura (Eds.), *Metacognition: Knowing about knowing* (pp. 185–205). Cambridge: Massachusetts Institute of Technology Press.

Black, D. S., Milam, J., & Sussman, S. (2009, September). Sitting-meditation interventions among youth: A review of treatment efficacy. *Pediatrics, 124*(3), 532–541.

Black, H. (1986). Assessment for learning. In D. L. Nuttall (Ed.), *Assessing educational achievement* (pp. 7–18). London: Falmer Press.

Black, P., Harrison, C., Lee, C., Marshall, B., & Wiliam, D. (2004). Working inside the black box: Assessment for learning in the classroom. *Phi Delta Kappan, 86*(1), 8–21.

Black, P. J., & Wiliam, D. (1998a). Assessment and classroom learning. *Assessment in Education: Principles, Policy and Practice, 5*(1), 7–73.

Black, P., & Wiliam, D. (1998b). *Inside the black box: Raising standards through classroom assessment.* London: King's College London School of Education.

Bloom, B. S. (1969). Some theoretical issues relating to educational evaluation. In H. G. Richey & R. W. Tyler (Eds.), *Educational evaluation: New roles, new means, pt. 2* (Vol. 68, pp. 26–50). Chicago: University of Chicago Press.

Boaler, J. (2002). *Experiencing school mathematics: Traditional and reform approaches to teaching and their impact on student learning.* Mahwah, NJ: Erlbaum.

Boekaerts, M. (1993). Being concerned with well being and with learning. *Educational Psychologist, 28*(2), 149–167.

Boekaerts, M. (2006). Self-regulation and effort investment. In K. A. Renninger & I. E. Sigel (Eds.), *Handbook of child psychology: Vol. 4. Child psychology in practice* (6th ed., pp. 345–377). New York: Wiley.

Bol, L., Campbell, K. D. Y., Perez, T., & Yen, C.-J. (2016). The effects of self-regulated learning training on community college students' metacognition and achievement in developmental math courses. *Community College Journal of Research and Practice, 40*(6), 480–495.

Boulet, M. M., Simard, G., & De Melo, D. (1990). Formative evaluation effects on learning music. *Journal of Educational Research, 84*(2), 119–125.

Broadfoot, P. M., Daugherty, R., Gardner, J., Gipps, C. V., Harlen, W., James, M. et al. (1999). *Assessment for learning: Beyond the black box.* Cambridge, England: University of Cambridge School of Education.

Brookhart, S. M. (2013). *How to create and use rubrics for formative assessment and grading.* Alexandria, VA: Association for Supervision and Curriculum Development. Accessed at www.ascd.org/publications/books /112001/chapters/What-Are-Rubrics-and-Why-Are-They-Important%C2%A2.aspx on April 1, 2017.

Brophy, J. (1981). Teacher praise: A functional analysis. *Review of Educational Research, 51*(1), 5–32.

Butler, D. L., & Winne, P. H. (1995). Feedback and self-regulated learning: A theoretical synthesis. *Review of Educational Research, 65*(3), 245–281.

Clarke, S. (2001). *Unlocking formative assessment.* London: Hodder & Stoughton.

Clarke, S. (2005). *Formative assessment in the secondary classroom.* London: Hodder & Stoughton.

Claxton, G. L. (1995). What kind of learning does self-assessment drive? Developing a "nose" for quality: Comments on Klenowski. *Assessment in Education: Principles, Policy and Practice, 2*(3), 339–343.

Cohen, E. G. (1994). Restructuring the classroom: Conditions for productive small groups. *Review of Educational Research, 64*(1), 1–35.

Cohen, E. G., & Lotan, R. A. (2014). *Designing groupwork: Strategies for the heterogeneous classroom* (3rd ed.). New York: Teachers College Press.

Corno, L. (2001). Volitional aspects of self-regulated learning. In B. J. Zimmerman & D. H. Schunk (Eds.), *Self-regulated learning and academic achievement: Theoretical perspectives* (2nd ed., pp. 191–225). Hillsdale, NJ: Erlbaum.

Cowie, B., & Bell, B. (1999). A model of formative assessment in science education. *Assessment in Education: Principles, Policy and Practice, 6*(1), 32–42.

Csikszentmihalyi, M. (1990). *Flow: The psychology of optimal experience.* New York: Harper & Row.

Davis, B. (1997). Listening for differences: An evolving conception of mathematics teaching. *Journal for Research in Mathematics Education, 28*(3), 355–376.

Dawes, L., Mercer, N., & Wegerif, R. (2000). *Thinking together: A programme of activities for developing speaking, listening and thinking skills for children aged 8–11.* Birmingham, England: Imaginative Minds.

Dillon, J. T. (1988). *Questioning and teaching: A manual of practice.* London: Croom Helm.

Dunlosky, J., Rawson, K. A., Marsh, E. J., Nathan, M. J., & Willingham, D. T. (2013). Improving students' learning with effective learning techniques: Promising directions from cognitive and educational psychology. *Psychological Science in the Public Interest, 14*(1), 4–58.

Dweck, C. S. (1975). The role of expectations and attributions in the alleviation of learned helplessness. *Journal of Personality and Social Psychology, 31*(4), 674–685.

Dweck, C. S. (2000). *Self-theories: Their role in motivation, personality and development.* Philadelphia: Psychology Press.

Dweck, C. S. (2006). *Mindset: The new psychology of success.* New York: Random House.

Educational Testing Service. (2002). *Standards for quality and fairness.* Princeton, NJ: Author.

Elawar, M. C., & Corno, L. (1985). A factorial experiment in teachers' written feedback on student homework: Changing teacher behaviour a little rather than a lot. *Journal of Educational Psychology, 77*(2), 162–173.

Even, R., & Tirosh, D. (1995). Subject-matter knowledge and the knowledge about students as sources of teacher presentations of the subject-matter. *Educational Studies in Mathematics, 29*(1), 1–20.

Flavell, J. H. (1976). Metacognitive aspects of problem solving. In L. B. Resnick (Ed.), *The nature of intelligence* (pp. 231–235). Hillsdale, NJ: Lawrence Erlbaum.

Formative. (2017). In *Merriam-Webster's online dictionary.* Accessed at www.merriam-webster.com/dictionary/formative on June 20, 2017.

Fredericks, A. D. (2005). *The complete idiot's guide to success as a teacher.* Indianapolis, IN: Alpha Books.

Fredericks, A. D. (2007). *The complete idiot's guide to teaching college: Engage and inspire your students from the very first day of class.* Indianapolis, IN: Alpha Books.

Good, T. L., & Grouws, D. A. (1975). *Process-product relationships in fourth grade mathematics classrooms* (Grant No. NEG-00-3-0123). Columbia: University of Missouri.

Hacker, D. J., Dunlosky, J., & Graesser, A. C. (Eds.). (1998). *Metacognition in educational theory and practice.* Mahwah, NJ: Lawrence Erlbaum.

Harlen, W., & Crick, R. D. (2002). *A systematic review of the impact of summative assessment and tests on students' motivation for learning.* London: EPPI-Centre, Social Science Research Unit, Institute of Education. Accessed at https://dspace.stir.ac.uk/bitstream/1893/19607/1/SysRevImpSummativeAssessment2002.pdf on April 28, 2017.

Hart, K. M., Brown, M. L., Kerslake, D., Küchemann, D., & Ruddock, G. (1985). *Chelsea diagnostic mathematics tests.* Windsor, England: National Foundation for Educational Research-Nelson.

Haug, B. S., & Ødegaard, M. (2015). Formative assessment and teachers' sensitivity to student responses. *International Journal of Science Education, 37*(4), 629–654.

Heid, M. K., Blume, G. W., Zbiek, R. M., & Edwards, B. S. (1999). Factors that influence teachers learning to do interviews to understand students' mathematical understandings. *Educational Studies in Mathematics, 37*(3), 223–249.

Hodgen, J., & Wiliam, D. (2006). *Mathematics inside the black box: Assessment for learning in the mathematics classroom.* London: NFER-Nelson.

Iberlin, J. M. (2017). *Cultivating mindfulness in the classroom.* Bloomington, IN: Solution Tree Press.

James, M. (1992). *Assessment for learning.* Paper presented at the annual conference of the Association for Supervision and Curriculum Development, New Orleans, LA.

Kahl, S. (2005). Where in the world are formative tests? Right under your nose! *Education Week, 25*(4), 11.

Keddie, N. (1971). Classroom knowledge. In M. F. D. Young (Ed.), *Knowledge and control: New directions for the sociology of education* (pp. 133–160). London: Collier-Macmillan.

Kluger, A. N., & DeNisi, A. (1996). The effects of feedback interventions on performance: A historical review, a meta-analysis, and a preliminary feedback intervention theory. *Psychological Bulletin, 119*(2), 254–284.

Kohn, A. (2006). The trouble with rubrics. *English Journal, 95*(4), 12–15.

Leahy, S., Lyon, C., Thompson, M., & Wiliam, D. (2005). Classroom assessment: Minute-by-minute and day-by-day. *Educational Leadership, 63*(3), 18–24. Accessed at www.ascd.org/publications/educational-leadership/nov05/vol63/num03/Classroom-Assessment@-Minute-by-Minute,-Day-by-Day.aspx on July 7, 2017.

Lewis, C. C. (2002). *Lesson study: A handbook of teacher-led instructional change.* Philadelphia: Research for Better Schools.

Lodico, M. G., Ghatala, E. S., Levin, J. R., Pressley, M., & Bell, J. A. (1983). The effects of strategy-monitoring training on children's selection of effective memory strategies. *Journal of Experimental Child Psychology, 35*(2), 263–277.

Looney, J. (Ed.). (2005). *Formative assessment: Improving learning in secondary classrooms.* Paris: Organisation for Economic Co-operation and Development.

Meiklejohn, J., Phillips, C., Freedman, M. L., Griffin, M. L., Biegel, G., Roach, A., et al. (2012). Integrating mindfulness training into K–12 education: Fostering the resilience of teachers and students. *Mindfulness, 3*(4), 291–307.

Mercer, N., Dawes, L., Wegerif, R., & Sams, C. (2004). Reasoning as a scientist: Ways of helping children to use language to learn science. *British Educational Research Journal, 30*(3), 359–377.

Metcalfe, J., Butterfield, B., Habeck, C., & Stern, Y. (2012). Neural correlates of people's hypercorrection of their false beliefs. *Journal of Cognitive Neuroscience, 24*(7), 1571–1583.

Mittler, P. J. (Ed.). (1973). *Assessment for learning in the mentally handicapped.* Edinburgh, Scotland: Churchill Livingstone.

National Council for Curriculum and Assessment. (2015). *Focus on learning: Learning intentions & success criteria.* Dublin, Ireland: Author. Accessed at www.juniorcycle.ie/NCCA_JuniorCycle/media/NCCA/Documents/Assessment/Ongoing%20Asssessment/Assessment-Workshop-1_Eng_April-15-2015.pdf on April 1, 2017.

Oláh, L. N., Lawrence, N. R., & Riggan, M. (2010). Learning to learn from benchmark assessment data: How teachers analyze results. *Peabody Journal of Education, 85*(2), 226–245.

Pomeroy, R. (2014). *Multiple-choice tests hinder critical thinking. Should they be used in science classes?* Accessed at www.realclearscience.com/blog/2014/02/multiple_choice_in_science_classes.html on August 26, 2017.

Popham, W. J. (2006). Phony formative assessments: Buyer beware! *Educational Leadership, 64*(3), 86–87.

Price-Mitchell, M. (2015). *Metacognition: Nurturing self-awareness in the classroom.* Accessed at www.edutopia.org/blog/8-pathways-metacognition-in-classroom-marilyn-price-mitchell on August 26, 2017.

Professional Development Service for Teachers. (2016). *Leaving certificate applied: Teacher handbook.* Dublin, Ireland: Author. Accessed at www.pdst.ie/sites/default/files/LCA%20Teacher%20Handbook.pdf on March 31, 2017.

Programme for International Student Assessment. (2007). *PISA 2006: Science competencies for tomorrow's world* (Vol. 1). Paris: Organisation for Economic Co-operation and Development.

Rempel, K. D. (2012). Mindfulness for children and youth: A review of the literature with an argument for school-based implementation. *Canadian Journal of Counselling and Psychotherapy, 46*(3), 201–220.

Rivkin, S. G., Hanushek, E. A., & Kain, J. F. (2005). Teachers, schools and academic achievement. *Econometrica, 73*(2), 417–458.

Rockoff, J. E. (2004). The impact of individual teachers on student achievement: Evidence from panel data. *American Economic Review, 94*(2), 247–252.

Rowe, M. B. (1974). Wait-time and rewards as instructional variables: Their influence on language, learning and fate control. *Journal of Research in Science Teaching, 11*(2), 81–94.

Ryle, G. (1949). *The concept of mind.* London: Hutchinson.

Sadler, D. R. (1989). Formative assessment and the design of instructional systems. *Instructional Science, 18*(2), 119–144.

Sadler, P. M. (1998). Psychometric models of student conceptions in science: Reconciling qualitative studies and distractor-driven assessment instruments. *Journal of Research in Science Teaching, 35*(3), 265–296.

Sanders, W. L., & Rivers, J. C. (1996). *Cumulative and residual effects of teachers on future student academic achievement.* Knoxville: University of Tennessee Value-Added Research and Assessment Center. Accessed at www.heartland.org/publications-resources/publications/cumulative-and-residual-effects-of-teachers-on-future-student-academic-achievement on August 21, 2010.

Saphier, J. (2005). Masters of motivation. In R. DuFour, R. Eaker, & R. DuFour (Eds.), *On common ground: The power of professional learning communities* (pp. 85–113). Bloomington, IN: Solution Tree Press.

Schacter, J. (2000). Does individual tutoring produce optimal learning? *American Educational Research Journal, 37*(3), 801–829.

Schwartz, B. (2003). *The paradox of choice: Why more is less.* New York: Ecco.

Scriven, M. (1967). The methodology of evaluation. In R. W. Tyler, R. M. Gagné, & M. Scriven (Eds.), *Perspectives of curriculum evaluation* (Vol. 1, pp. 39–83). Chicago: RAND.

Siegel, D. J. (2007). *The mindful brain: Reflection and attunement in the cultivation of well-being.* New York: Norton.

Shanker, S. (2013). *Calm, alert and learning: Classroom strategies for self-regulation.* North York, ON: Pearson Education Canada.

Shepard, L. A. (2008). Formative assessment: Caveat emptor. In C. A. Dwyer (Ed.), *The future of assessment: Shaping teaching and learning* (pp. 279–303). Mahwah, NJ: Lawrence Erlbaum.

Shepard, L. A., Hammerness, K., Darling-Hammond, L., Rust, F., Snowden, J. B., Gordon, E. et al. (2005). Assessment. In L. Darling-Hammond & J. Bransford (Eds.), *Preparing teachers for a changing world: What teachers should learn and be able to do* (pp. 275–326). San Francisco: Jossey-Bass.

Silver, D. (2012). *The power of teachers' words.* Accessed at www.middleweb.com/3995/the-power-of-what-teachers-say/ on August 26, 2017.

Simmons, M., & Cope, P. (1993). Angle and rotation: Effects of differing types of feedback on the quality of response. *Educational Studies in Mathematics, 24*(2), 163–176.

Slavin, R. E., Hurley, E. A., & Chamberlain, A. (2003). Cooperative learning and achievement. In W. M. Reynolds & G. J. Miller (Eds.), *Handbook of psychology: Educational psychology* (Vol. 7, pp. 177–198). Hoboken, NJ: Wiley.

Spencer, J. (2016). *Making learning flow.* Bloomington, IN: Solution Tree Press.

Stevens, R. J., & Slavin, R. E. (1995). Effects of a cooperative learning approach in reading and writing on academically handicapped and nonhandicapped students. *Elementary School Journal, 95*(3), 241–262.

Stiggins, R. J. (2001). *Student-involved classroom assessment* (3rd ed.). Upper Saddle River, NJ: Prentice Hall.

Stiggins, R. J. (2005). From formative assessment to assessment FOR learning: A path to success in standards-based schools. *Phi Delta Kappan, 87*(4), 324–328.

Tobin, K. (1987). The role of wait time in higher cognitive level learning. *Review of Educational Research, 57*(1), 69–95.

Webb, N. M. (1991). Task-related verbal interaction and mathematics learning in small groups. *Journal for Research in Mathematics Education, 22*(5), 366–389.

White, M. A. (1971). The view from the student's desk. In M. L. Silberman (Ed.), *The experience of schooling* (pp. 337–345). New York: Holt, Rinehart and Winston.

Wiener, N. (1948). *Cybernetics: Or control and communication in the animal and the machine.* Cambridge: Massachusetts Institute of Technology Press.

Wiggins, G. (2012). Seven keys to effective feedback. *Educational Leadership, 70*(1), 10–16.

Wiliam, D. (2014, April). *Formative assessment and contingency in the regulation of learning experiences.* Paper presented at Toward a Theory of Classroom Assessment as the Regulation of Learning Symposium at the annual meeting of the American Educational Research Association, Philadelphia.

Wiliam, D. (2018). *Embedded formative assessment* (2nd ed.). Bloomington, IN: Solution Tree Press.

Wiliam, D., & Black, P. J. (1996). Meanings and consequences: A basis for distinguishing formative and summative functions of assessment? *British Educational Research Journal, 22*(5), 537–548.

Winne, P. H. (1996). A metacognitive view of individual differences in self-regulated learning. *Learning and Individual Differences, 8*(4), 327–353.

Wylie, C., & Wiliam, D. (2006, April). *Diagnostic questions: Is there value in just one?* Paper presented at the annual meeting of the American Educational Research Association and the National Council on Measurement in Education, San Francisco.

Zimmerman, B. J. (2002). Becoming a self-regulated learner: An overview. *Theory Into Practice, 41*(2), 64–70.

Index

A

ABCD cards, 46

all-student response systems, 44–48

Arter, J. A., 26

Assessment Reform Group (ARG), 8

assessments

    See also formative assessment

    for learning, 8, 9

Ausubel, D. P., 51

B

backward design, 13, 19

Bandura, A., 88

Bell, B., 7

Bennett, R. E., 8

Black, P. J., 7, 65

Bloom, B., 6

Boekaerts, M., 87, 89

Brookhart, S. M., 26

C

category error, 7

Chamberlain, A., 71

choose-swap-choose, 30

Clarke, S., 27, 30, 32

Claxton, G. L., 24

co-construction of learning intentions, 21–22

cognitive elaboration, 73

Cohen, E. G., 74

collaborative learning. *See* cooperative learning

constructive feedback, 57

cooperative learning

    C3B4ME, 74–75

    effectiveness of, 71, 73–74

    elaborated explanations, 74

    end-of-topic questions, 76

    error classification, 76

    group-based test preparation, 78

    group goals, 73

    group rewards, 73

groups, half-ability, 74

homework help board, 75–76, 77

individual accountability, 73

inventory of current practices, 71, 72

I-you-we checklist, 78, 80

peer tutoring, 75

planning template, 82, 101

preflight checklist, 78, 79

student reporter, 76

techniques, 74–80

two stars and a wish, 76, 78

Cowie, B., 7

Csikszentmihalyi, M., 87–88

C3B4ME, 74–75

D

data-push formative assessment, 13

Davis, B., 50

decision-pull formative assessment, 13

Deming, W. E., 8

DeNisi, A. S., 59

Dweck, C. S., 61–62

E

elaborated explanations, 74

elaboration time, 44

Embedded Formative Assessment (2nd ed.) (Wiliam), 1, 57

engagement techniques. *See* high-engagement, 37

error classification, 76

evaluative listening, 50–51

exit passes, 30, 31, 47–48

F

feedback

constructive, 57

engineering test and, 57–59

focused, 67

formative, 65–68

future actions based on, 65–68

inventory of current practices, 57, 58

learning goals and, 68

loop, 58–59, 60

mindset, growth versus fixed, 61–62, 63

planning template, 69, 100

praise, 62–63

reactions to, 59, 61–63

scaffolded, 63–65

three questions, 66–67

types of, 57

use of term, 57–59

fist to five, 44

fixed mindset, 61–62

Flavell, J. H., 87

Flow: The Psychology of Optimal Experience (Csikszentmihalyi), 87–88

formative assessment

data-push, 13

decision-pull, 13

definitions of, 5–10

design, 11–13

evolution of, 6–8

inventory of current practices, 11, 12

preassessment of, 3–5

short-cycle, 15

strategies of, 13–14

formative evaluation, 6

G

Good, T. L., 62

group-based test preparation, 78

group goals, 73

group rewards, 73

groups, half-ability, 74

Grouws, D. A., 62

growth mindset, 61–62, 63

H

high-engagement classroom, 37

all-student response systems, 44–48

impact of, 39

no hands up, 39–43

wait time, 43–44

homework

help board, 75–76, 77

peer improvement of, 75

Hurley, E. A., 71

hypercorrection effect, 90

I

Inside the Black Box: Raising Standards Through Classroom Assessment (Black and Wiliam), 65

instruction, use of term, 6–7

interpretive listening, 51

I-you-we checklist, 78, 80

J

James, M., 8

K

Kahl, S., 7

Keddie, N., 19

Kluger, A. N., 59

Kohn, A., 26

L

learned helplessness, 61

learning

context of, 30, 32

linking teaching with, 14–15

self-regulated, 85–90

use of term, 10

learning, evidence of

See also questioning techniques

inventory of current practices, 37, 38

planning template, 54–55, 99

learning goals, feedback and, 68

learning intentions
>   *See also* success criteria
>   clarifying, 19–33, 98
>   co-construction of, 21–22
>   confused versus clarified, examples of, 30, 32
>   defined, 19
>   inventory of current practices, 17–18
>   language, official versus student-friendly, 19–20, 22–23
>   planning template, 98
>   timing of sharing, 20–21
learning logs, 92, 94
learning portfolios, 91–92, 93
letter corners, 46
listening, evaluative and interpretive, 50–51

M

McTighe, J., 26
memory, 90
metacognition, 87
mindset, growth versus fixed, 61–62, 63
Mittler, P., 8
motivation, 73, 87–89
multiple-choice questions, 46, 51

N

no hands up, 39–43
nose for quality, 24–25

O

Organisation for Economic Co-operation and Development (OECD), 7

P

Paradox of Choice: Why More Is Less, The (Schwartz), 2
pedagogy, 6
peer tutoring, 75
personalization, 73
pose-pause-pounce-bounce, 39–40
praise, 62–63
preflight checklist, 78, 79
Price-Mitchell, M., 87
process criteria, 26–28
Professional Development Service for Teachers, 19

Q

questioning techniques
>   ABCD cards, 46
>   all-student response systems, 44–48
>   end-of-topic, 76
>   exit passes, 30, 31, 47–48
>   high-quality, 48–51
>   multiple-choice, 46, 51
>   no hands up, 39–43
>   Popsicle sticks, use of, 40
>   pose-pause-pounce-bounce, 39–40
>   self-reports, 44, 46

shells, 52–54

wait time, 43–44, 45

whiteboards, mini, 47

questions

end-of-topic, 76

reasons for asking, 39

shells, 52–54

as statements, 52

R

Raven's Progressive Matrices, 39

Reeves, D., 65

rubrics, task-specific versus generic
scoring, 25–26

Ryle, G., 7

S

Sadler, D. R., 19

Saphier, J., 64

scaffolded feedback, 63–65

Schacter, J., 73

Schwartz, B., 2

Scriven, M., 6

self-assessment

colored cups, 91

learning logs, 92, 94

learning portfolios, 91–92, 93

red or green lights, 91

planning template, 95, 102

techniques, 90–95

traffic lights, 91

self-efficacy, 88

self-regulated learning

inventory of current practices, 85,
86

metacognition, 87

motivation, 73, 87–89

self-reports, 44, 46

self-testing, 90

short-cycle formative assessment, 15

Slavin, R., 71

social cohesion, 73

Stiggins, R. J., 8

storage strength, 90

student-friendly language, 19–20,
22–23

student reporter, 76

student self-assessment. See
self-assessment

success criteria

process criteria and, 26–28

role of, 24–25

rubrics and, 25–27

student evaluation of other
students' work, 28–30, 31

summative evaluation, 6

T

teacher quality, impact of, 2

teaching, linking learning with, 14–15

thinking thumbs, 44

Thinking Together program, 39

think-pair-share, 52

three questions, 66–67

TIB (this is because), 30

traffic lights, 91

trailing edge, 73

two stars and a wish, 76, 78

W

wait time, 43–44, 45

WALT (we are learning to), 30

White, M. A., 21–22

whiteboards, mini, 47

Wiener, N., 58

Wiliam, D., 1, 2, 6, 7, 8, 9, 10, 11, 13,
        14, 19, 22, 26, 28, 30, 39, 40,
        43, 46, 48, 51, 53, 57, 62, 64,
        65, 66, 68, 73, 74, 75, 76, 78,
        90

Wylie, C., 11, 13

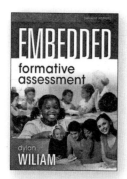

Embedded Formative Assessment, Second Edition
Dylan Wiliam
The second edition of this best-selling resource presents new research, insights, examples, and formative assessment techniques teachers can immediately apply in their classrooms. Updated examples and templates help teachers elicit evidence of learning, provide meaningful feedback, and empower students to take ownership of their education.
BKF790

Content, *Then* Process
Featuring Dylan Wiliam
In this striking keynote, Dr. Wiliam encourages the building of teacher learning communities (TLCs). He provides practical techniques to embed formative assessment in regular classroom practice and illustrates how TLCs can be established and sustained within schools and districts to support teachers.
DVF058

Essential Assessment
Cassandra Erkens, Tom Schimmer, and Nicole Dimich Vagle
Discover how to use the power of assessment to instill hope, efficacy, and achievement in your students. With this research-based resource, you'll explore six essential tenets of assessment—assessment purpose, communication of assessment results, accurate interpretation, assessment architecture, instructional agility, and student investment—that will help deepen your understanding of assessment to not only meet standards but also enhance students' academic success and self-fulfillment.
BKF752

Instructional Agility
Cassandra Erkens, Tom Schimmer, and Nicole Dimich Vagle
This highly practical resource empowers readers to become instructionally agile—moving seamlessly among instruction, formative assessment, and feedback—to enhance student engagement, proficiency, and ownership of learning. Each chapter concludes with reflection questions that assist readers in determining next steps.
BKF764

Simplifying Common Assessment
Kim Bailey and Chris Jakicic
Built on the process featured in *Common Formative Assessment: A Toolkit for PLCs at Work*™, this book demonstrates how educators can develop effective and efficient assessments. The authors simplify assessment development to give teacher teams the confidence to write and use team-designed common formative assessments that help ensure all students master essential skills and concepts.
BKF750

GL⬤BAL **PD**

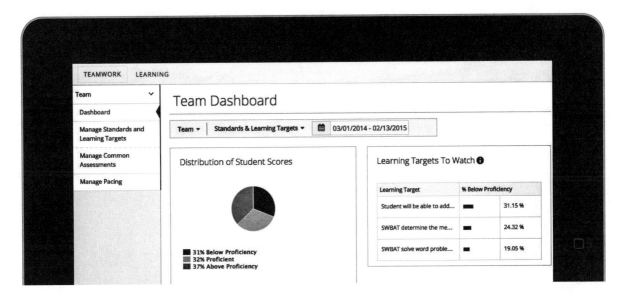

The **Power to Improve**
Is in Your Hands

Global PD gives educators focused and goals-oriented training from top experts. You can rely on this innovative online tool to improve instruction in every classroom.

- Get unlimited, on-demand access to guided video and book content from top Solution Tree authors.

- Improve practices with personalized virtual coaching from PLC-certified trainers.

- Customize learning based on skill level and time commitments.